Richard Laffes

An Italian Voyage

A Complete Journey through Italy

Richard Laffes

An Italian Voyage
A Complete Journey through Italy

ISBN/EAN: 9783742823618

Manufactured in Europe, USA, Canada, Australia, Japa

Cover: Foto ©Andreas Hilbeck / pixelio.de

Manufactured and distributed by brebook publishing software (www.brebook.com)

Richard Laffes

An Italian Voyage

AN
Italian Voyage,
OR, A
Compleat *JOURNEY*
THROUGH
ITALY.

· In Two Parts. ·

With the *Characters* of the People, and the Description of the Chief Towns, Churches, Monasteries, Tombs, Libraries, Pallaces, Villa's, Gardens, Pictures, Statues and Antiquities.

AS ALSO,

Of the Interest, Government, Riches, Force, &c. of all the Princes.

With Instructions concerning *TRAVEL*.

By *Richard Lassels*, Gent. the Second Edition with large Additions, by a Modern hand.

LONDON,
Printed for *Richard Wellington*, at the *Lute* in St. *Paul*'s Church-Yard, and *B. Barnard* Linnet, at the *Cross-Keys*, in St. *Martins-Lane*, near *Long-Acre*. 1697.

A PREFACE.
TO THE
READER,
CONCERNING
𝕮𝖗𝖆𝖛𝖊𝖑𝖑𝖎𝖓𝖌.

WHEN I first set Pen to Paper ⲧ handle this subject, I had not the least thought of the *Press*; nor of erecting my self into an *Authour*. I only discharged my memory hastily of some things which I had seen in *Italy*; and wrapt up that untimely *Embryo* in five sheets of Paper, for the use of a Noble person, who set me that Task. Yet this *Embryo* liking the person for whom it was conceived, obliged me to lick it over again, and bring it into better form. Second thoughts, and succeeding Voyages into *Italy*, have finished it at last, and have made it what it is; *A Compleat Voyage,* and an exact *Itinerary* through *Italy*

And here I thought to have drawn bridle and refted, after fo long a Journey; when a Learned Friend having purufed this my Defcription of *Italy*, defired much to fee a Preface to it of my fafhion, and Concerning Travelling. I could refufe nothing to fuch a Friend; and have done it here willingly, both for my own, and my Countries fake.

For my own fake; to pre-excufe fome things in my Book, which fome perchance may diflike.

For fome, I fear will quarrel with my *Englifh*, and juftly, feeing three long Voyages into *Flanders*, fix into *France*, five into *Italy*, one into *Germany* and *Holland*, have made me live half of my life-time in Foreign Countries, to the difturbance of my own Language: Yet, if I bring not home fine Language, I bring home fine Things; and I have feen great Ladies, both in *France* and *England*, buy fine things of *Chimney-fweepers* and *Pedlars*, though they fpake but courfe *Lombard* Language, and grofs *Scotch*.

Others perchance will find fault, that I write merrily fometimes: And why not? Seeing I write to young Men, and for them; and mirth is never fo lawfull as in Travelling: where it fhortens long miles, and fweetens bad ufage; that is, makes a bad dinner go down, and a bad horfe go on.

Others

Others will say, That I fill my Book with too much *Latin*: But these must be minded, that I am writing of the *Latin* Country; and that I am carving for *Scholars*, who can digest solid bits, having good stomachs.

Others will say, I jeer now and then: And would any man have me go through so many divers Countries, and praise all I see? Or in earnest, do not some things deserve to be jeered, when things cannot be cured but by jeering: *Jeering*, saith *Tertullian*, *is a duty*; and I think the *Cynick* Philosophers struck as great a blow at Vice, as the *Stoicks*.

Others will say, I change style often, and sometimes run smoothly, and sometimes joltingly: True, I travelled not always upon smooth ground, and pacing horses: *Swifferland* and *Savoy* are much different from *Campania* and *Lombardy*; and it's one thing to describe a Pleasant Garden, another thing to describe a Venerable Cathedral: and if in the one, and the other, we have several looks, much more ought we to have several words in describing them.

Others will say, I affect a world of exotick words not yet naturalized in *England*: No, I affect them not; I cannot avoid them: for who can speak of *Statues*, but he must speak of *Niches*; or of *Churches*,

A 2   Wrought

Wrought *Tombs*, or in-laid *Tables*, but he muſt ſpeak of *Cupola*'s; of *baſſo relievo*; and of *pietre commeſſe*? If any Man underſtand them not, it's his fault, not mine.

Others will ſay, I hunt too much after Ceremonies and Church-antiquities. No, I only meet them. And as a man cannot ſpeak of *Hercules*, but he muſt ſpeak of *Clubs*, of *Combats*, of *Labours* and *Victories*: ſo I cannot ſpeak of *Rome* as it is now, but I muſt ſpeak of Relicks, Ceremonies and Religion. Yet I believe, I give my Reader no very unfiniſh'd draught of prophane *Antiquities, Maſquerades, Shews, Dreſſings* and *Paſtimes*.

Others, in fine, will ſay, that I do but a thing done already; ſeeing others have Written of this Subject in *Engliſh*. Well; if others have Written upon this ſub-
Mr. *Way-* ject, why may not I? They did the beſt
cup. they could, I believe: but they drew not
Mr. *Ray-* up the Ladder after them. Some write
mond. much of *Italy*, and ſay little: And others write little, and leave out much: I impute to the ones writing out of old. And if theſe Ingenious Gentlemen have painted out *Italy* in *buſto* only, and *profile*: why may not I endeavour to paint her out at *full face*, and *at her full length*? If they, like ancient Statuaries, have repreſented *Italy* unto us like a naked *Image*, I may perhaps be allow'd to ſay that I have ſet
her

her out in all her best *Attire* and *Jewels*. And thus much for my self.

For my Country: To read to my Country-men two profitable *Lessons*: The first, *Of the Profit of Travelling*: The second, *Of Travelling with Profit*.

1. For the first, to wit, *the Profit of Travelling*; it's certain, that if this world be a great *Book*, as St. *Augustine* calls it, none study this great *Book* so much as the Traveller. They that never stir from home, read only one Page of this *Book*; and, like the dull fellow in *Pliny*, who could never learn to count farther than five, they dwell always upon one Lesson. They are like an acquaintance of mine, who had always a Book indeed lying open upon a Desk; but it was observed that it lay always open at one and the same place, and by long custom, could lie open no where else. He then that will know much out of this great Book, the World, must read much in it: and as *Ulysses* is set forth by *Homer* as the wisest of all the *Græcians*, because he had travelled much, and had seen *multorum hominum mores & Urbes, the Cities and Customs of many Men*: So his Son *Telemachus* is held for a very shallow-witted man: and *Homer* gives the reason, because his Mother *Penelope*, instead of sending him abroad to see Foreign Countries, had always kept him at home, and so made him

The profit of Travel. Aug.

him a meer *Onocephalus* and a homeling *Mammacuth*. So true is the saying of *Seneca*, that, *Imper ant est animal homo, & fine magna experientia rerum, fi circumfcribatur Natalis foli fine.*

2. Travelling preferves my young Nobleman from furfeiting of his Parents, and weans him from the dangerous fondnefs of his Mother. It teacheth him wholefome hardfhip; to lie in beds that are none of his acquaintance; to fpeak to men he never faw before; to travel in the morning before day; and in the evening when 'tis dark, to endure any horfe and weather, as well as any meat and drink. Whereas the Country Gentleman that never Travelled, can fcarce go to *London* without making his Will, at leaft without wetting his Handkerchief. And what generous Mother will not fay to her fon with that Ancient; *Mola tibi male effe, quam molliter: I had rather thou shouldst be fick, than foft?* Indeed the Coral-Tree, is neither hard nor red, till taken out of the Sea, its native home. And I have read, that many of the old *Romans* put out their Children to be Nurfed abroad by *Lacedæmonian* Nurfes, till they were three years old; then they put them to their Uncles, till feven, or ten; then they fent them into *Tofcany* to be inftructed in Religion; and at laft into *Greece* to ftudy Philofophy.

Sence.

3. Tra-

3. Travelling takes my young Nobleman four notches lower in his self-conceit and pride. For, whereas the Country Lord, that never saw any body but his Fathers Tenants and Mr. Parson; and never read any thing but *John Stow*, and *Speed*, thinks the Lands-end to be the Worlds-end; and that all solid greatness, next unto a great Pasty, consists in a great Fire, and a good Estate. Whereas my Travelling young Lord, who hath seen so many greater Men and Estates than his own, comes home far more modest and civil to his inferiours, and far less puft up with the empty conceit of his own greatness. Indeed nothing cured *Alcibiades* his pride so much as to see in a Map (shewed him for the nonce by *Socrates*) that his House and Lands, of which he was so proud, either appeared there not at all, or only a little Spot or Dab; and *nemo in pusillo magnus*.

4. Travelling takes off, in some sort, that aboriginal curse, which was laid upon mankind even almost at the beginning of the World; I mean, the confusion of Tongues: which is such a curse indeed, that it makes Men who are of one kind, and made to be sociable, so strangely to fly one another, that as great S. *Austin* saith, a Man had rather be with his Dog, than with a Man whose Language he understands not. Nay, this

this diverſity of Language, makes the wiſeſt Man paſs for a Fool in a ſtrange Country, and the beſt Man, for an excommunicated Perſon, whoſe Converſation all Men avoid. Now travelling takes of this curſe, and this moral excommunication; by making us learn many languages, and converſe freely with people of other Countries.

5. Travelling makes us acquainted with a world of our kindred we never ſaw before, For, ſeeing we are all come from one man at firſt, and conſequently all a-kin to one another; its but a reaſonable thing, that a Man ſhould once at leaſt in his life time, make a Journey into Foreign Countries, to ſee his Relations, and viſit this kindred: having always this ſaying of young *Joſeph* in his Mouth ; *quæro fratres meos*.

6. Travelling enables a Man much for his Countries Service. It makes the Merchant rich, by ſhewing him what abounds, and wants in other Countries; that ſo he may know what to import, what to export. It makes the *Mechanick* come loaden home with a world of experimental knowledge for the improving of his Trade. It makes the *Field Officer,* a knowing Leader of an Army, by teaching him where an Army in Foreign Countries, can march ſecurely, paſs Rivers eaſily,

fily, incamp safely, avoid Ambufcadoes and narrow paffages difcreetly, and retreat orderly. It makes the *Common Soldier* play the Spy well, by making him fpeak the Enemies Language perfectly, that fo mingling with them, he may find their defigns, and crofs their Plots. In fine, it makes a *Nobleman* fit for the nobleft Employment; that is, to be *Ambaſſador* abroad for his King in Foreign Countries, and carry about with him the King's *Perſon*, which he reprefents, and his King's *Word*, which he engageth.

7. Travelling brings a Man a world of particular profits. It contents the Mind with the rare difcourfes we hear from Learned Men, as the Queen of *Sheba* was ravifhed at the Wifdom of *Solomon*. It makes an Ingenious Man much the wifer by making him fee the good and the bad in others. Hence the Wifeman faith; *Sapiens in terram alienigenarum gentium pertranfiet : bona enim & mala in hominibus tentabit*. It makes a Man think himfelf at home every where, and fmile at unjuft *exile* : It makes him welcome home again to his *Neighbours*, fought after by his *Betters*, and liftened unto with admiration by his *Inferiours*. It makes him fit ftill in his old age with fatisfaction; and travel over the World again in his *Chair* and *Bed* by difcourfe and thoughts.

In

In fine, it's an excellent *Commentary* upon Histories; and no Man understands *Livy* and *Cæsar*, *Guicciardin* and *Monluc*, like him, who hath made exactly the *Grand Tour* of *France*, and the *Giro* of *Italy*.

8. Travelling makes my young Nobleman return home again to his Country like a *blessing Sun*. For as the *Sun*, who hath been Travelling about the World these five thousand and odd years, not only enlightens those places which he visits, but also enricheth them with all sorts of *Fruits* and *Metals*: So, the Nobleman by long travelling, having enlightened his understanding with fine notions, comes home like a glorious *Sun*, and doth not only shine bright in the Firmament of his Country, the *Parliament-House*; but also blesseth his inferiours with the powerfull influence if his knowing Spirit.

9. In fine, Examples (the best Philosophy) shew us, that the greatest Princes *Europe* hath seen, these many years, to wit, *Charles the V.* and the *King of Sweeden*, *Gustavus Adolphus*, were both of them great Travellers; the first had been twice in *England*, as often in *Africk*, four times in *France*, six times in *Spain*, seven times in *Italy*, and nine into *Germany*: The second had travelled *incognito* (as M. *Watts* writes of him) into *Holland*, *France*,

Strada de Billo Belg.

France, *Italy* and *Germany*, in his youth; which made him say afterwards to the French Ambassador *Mareschal Breze*, in a kind of threatning way, that he knew the way to *Paris*, as well as to *Stockholme*. Add to this, that the wisest and greatest among the ancient *Philosophers*, *Plato*, *Pythagoras*, *Anaxagoras*, *Anacharsis*, *Appollonius*, *Architas*, and *Pittacus*, (which last left his supream Command of *Mytelen* to travel) were all great travellers; and that St. *Hierom* (who being no *Bishop*, and consequently not obliged to residence) having travelled into *France*, *Italy*, *Greece*, and the *Holy Land*, purchased to himself such rare acquisitions of Learning by his Travels and Languages, that among all the ancient Fathers and Doctors, the Church in her Collect on his day, calls him only, *Doctorem maximum*, the greatest *Doctor*. And so much for the *profit of Travelling*.

Now for as much as concerns the second *Lesson*, to wit, *The Travelling with Profit*, divers things are to be taken notice of; some by the Parents or Guardians of those that travel; others by the Travellers themselves.

As for the Parents their greatest care ought to be of providing their Children (I speak to Men of high condition) a good Governour, to travel with them, and have

The Travelling with profit.

a care of their Perſons and breeding: that is, play the part of the *Archangel Raphael* to young *Toby*, and *Lead them ſafe abroad, and bring them ſafe home*: *Ego Janum ducam & reducam fillium tuum*. *Tob.* 5. v. 20. And here I could wiſh indeed that Parents could be as happy in their choice, and find Men Angels for Governours to their Children, upon condition they ſhould requite them, as young *Toby* offered to requite the *Archangel* his Governour, whom he took to be a Man. For the education of Children is a thing of that high concern to the Commonwealth, that in this, Parents ſhould ſpare no coſt whatſoever; but rather imitate the old *Lacedæmonians*; who took more care of their Youth, than of any thing elſe in their Commonwealth. Infomuch, that when *Antigonus* asked of them fifty young Youths for Hoſtages, they anſwered him, that they had rather give him twice as many made Men. Seeing then young youths are the future hopes of Famalies and Commonwealths, their education ought not to be committed but to Men of great Parts and excellent Breeding. For I have always thought, that a young Noblemans Train ought to be like his Cloths, His Lacqueys and Footmen are like his Galoſhoos, which he leaves at the door of thoſe he Viſits: His *Valets de Chambre*

Chambre, are like his Night-Gown, which he never useth but in his Chamber; and leaves them there when he goes in Visits: His Gentleman Attendants are like his several rich Suits, which he wears not all at once, but now one, now another, and sometimes none at all of them: His Groom is like his Riding-Cloak, and never appears near him but upon the Road: But his Governour is like his Shirt, which is always next unto his Skin and Person; and therefore as young Noblemen are curious to have their Shirts of the finest Linen: so should they have their Governours of the finest thread, and the best spun Men that can be found. Hence the Ancients, as they were careful in honouring the Memory of those that had been Governours to great Heroes, as of *Chiron*, Governour of *Hercules, Jason, Paris, Achilles*, and other brave Heroes; *Miscus*, Governour of *Ulysses*; *Eudorus* of *Patroclus*; *Dares* of *Hector*; *Epitides* of *Julus*; *Connidas* of *Theseus*; all of them choice men: So they were for choosing the finest men for that great Employment, to be their Childrens Governours; that is in their Language, *Custodes & comites juventutis Principum & magnatum.* For not every honest and vertuous Man (as some Parents think) is fit for this Employment: Those parts indeed would do well in a Steward,

a and

The Character of a good Governor. and a Sollicitor; but many things else, besides these, must concur to make up a good Governour. I would have him then to be not only a Vertuous Man, but a *Virtuoso* too, not only an honest Man, but a Man of honour too: not only a Gentleman born, but a gentile Man also by breeding: a Man not only comely of Person by nature; but gracefull also by art in his Garbs and Behaviour; a good Scholar, but no meer Scholar: a Man that hath travelled much in Foreign Countries, but yet no fickle-headed Man; a Man of a stout Spirit, but yet of a discreet Tongue, and who knows rather to wave quarrels prudently, than to maintain them stoutly; a Man cheetfull in conversation, yet fearfull to offend others; a Man of that Prudence, as to teach his Pupil rather to be wise than witty; and of that Example of life, that his deeds may make his Pupil believe his words: In fine, I would have him to be an *Englishman*, no *Stranger*. I speak not this out of an envy to Strangers, but out of a love to my own Country-men. For I have known divers *English* Gentlemen much wronged abroad by their Governours that were Strangers. Some I have known that led their Pupil to *Geneva*, where they got some *French* Language, but lost all their true *English* Allegiance

and

and respect to Monarchy; others I have known, who, being married and having their settlements and interest lying at *Saumur*, kept young Gentlemen there all the time they were abroad; and made their Parents in *England* believe, that all good breeding was in that poor Town, where their Wives were breeding Children. Others, I have known, who having their Mistresses in the Country, perswaded their young Pupils, Men of great Birth, that it was fine living in a Country House, that is fine carrying a Gun upon their necks and walking a foot: Others have been observed to sell thir Pupils to Masters of Exercises, and to have made 'em believe that the worst Academies were the best, because they were the best to the cunning Governour, who had ten pound a Man for every one he could draw thither: Others I have known who would have married their Pupils in *France*, without their Parents knowledge; and have sacrificed their great Trust, to their sordid Avarice: Others I have known who have locked their Pupils in a Chamber with a wanton Woman, and taken the Key away with them. Nay, this I can say more, that of all those Strangers that I have known Governours to young Noblemen of *England* (and I have known seven or eight) I never knew one of them to be a Gentleman

tleman born; but for the most part, they were needy bold Men, whose chief parts were, their own Language and some *Latin*, and whose chief aim was, to serve themselves, not their Pupils.

But to return again to our Subject; the Parent having found out such a Governour for his Son, as we have described here above, he must resign over unto him his full Authority, and command his Son to obey him: otherwise let the Governour be the wisest and the most Compleat Man in the World, if his Pupil do not obey him, and follow his Counsel, all will go wrong. I have seen great disorders befal for want of this. Hence I have often thought of great *Clemens Alexandrinus*, who saith wisely, That our *Saviour Christ* is the only true Preceptor or Governour, because he cannot only give the best Instructions to young Men, but also can give them grace to execute those instructions: whereas other Governours (*Cassandra* like) telling their Pupils many excellent Truths, are not believed by them; nor can they force their inclination to execute them, except the Parents commands come in to their assistance; and it is but reasonable, that as Governours are the Seconds of Parents, in the breeding of their Children, so Parents should second Governours too, in making
their

their Children obey them. And so much for the Parents Care.

For the Son's Care, it must be this. First to take a view of *England* before he enter into Foreign Countries. This will enure him to travel, to see company, to observe Towns and Rarities, and sharpen his appetite for Foreign Curiosities. I would wish him withal in travelling over *England*, to fall in, as often as he can, with the Judges in their Circuits, not only to see how his Country is Governed in point of Judicature; but also to see the Gentry of several Countries, who flock to great Towns in the Assize week. It would be also profitable to him, to cast to be at all the chief Horse-races, where he will easily see also the Gentry of the several Counties in a compendious View. Having thus seen his own Country in a Summers space, and having got his Majesties Licence to travel beyond the Seas (in which Licence I would wish this clause were inserted, That all young Gentlemen should, at their return, present themselves to his Majesty, to give him an Account of their Travels and Observations) I would have him depart *England* about the beginning of *October*.

2. At his going out of *England*, let him take his right aim; that is, let him aim altogether at his Profit, and not at his

his pleasures only. I have known many *Englishmen*, who for want of right aiming, have missed the white of Breeding, whole Heavens breadth. For some in travelling, aim at nothing but to get loose from their Parents, or Schoolmasters, and to have the fingering of a pretty Allowance; and these Men, when they come into *France*, care for seeing no Court, but the Tennis-Court; delight in seeing no Balls but Tennis-Balls; and forsake any Company, to toss whole days together with a tattered *Marker* in the *Tripot*.

Others desire to go into *Italy*, only because they hear there are fine Courtisans in *Venice*; and as the Queen of the *Amazons*, in *Justin*, went thirteen days Journey out of her Country, only to have a Nights Lodging with *Alexander the Great*; so these Men travel a whole month together to *Venice*, for a Nights Lodging with an impudent Woman. And thus by a false aiming at breeding abroad, they return with those Diseases which hinder them from breeding at home.

Others travel abroad, as our Ship-Boys do into the *Indies*: for whiles these Boys might bring home Jewels, Pearls, and many other things of value, they bring home nothing but Firecanes, Parots, and Monkeys; so our young Travellers, whiles they might bring home many rich observations,

vations, for the Governing themselves, and others, bring home nothing but Firecanes, that is a hotspur humour, that takes Fire at every word, and talk of nothing but Duels, Seconds, and Esclaircissements; or else Parots, that is, come loaden home with Ribons and Feathers of all Colours like Parots, and with a few borrowed Complements in their Mouths, which make them talk like Parots, or else Monkeys, that is some affected Cringes, Shrugs, and such like Apish Behaviour.

3. At his embarking let him have a special care not to carry himself abroad with himself in travelling: Many Men, saith *Seneca*, return home no better than they went out, because they take themselves along with themselves in Travelling: and as a Man in a Fever, finds himself no better than he was, by changing his Bed, because he carries his Fever with him Wheresoever he lies: so many young Men return home tired and dirtied, but not better and wiser, because they carried abroad their bad Customs and Manners with them. I would then that my young Traveller should leave behind him all wilfulness and stubborness; all tenderness, and seeking his ease too much; all effeminateness and delicateness; all Boyish Tricks with Hands or Mouth, and mocking of others; all delight of being accoun-

ted best Man in the Company; all familia-
ry with Servants, and mean Men; all
Taverns, and intemperancy of eating and
drinking; having that saying of *Seneca*
often in his mouth and mind; *Major sum
& ad majora natus, quam ut municipium
sim corporis mei*: *I am a greater Man and born
to greater things, than that I should yield
my self a slave to my Body.* In fine, I
would have him imitate that young Gentleman of whom S. *Ambrose* speaks; who
returning home from Foreign Travels,
and meeting with his old Mistress, a
Wanton Woman, seemed not to know
her; whereat she wondring, told him
that she was such an one; it may
be so, said he, but *I am no more I*. A
rare Apothegm; which I would wish
my young Traveller to take for his Motto, as well as this young Man for his Example.

4. Being thus got out of *England*, its
a great question into what Country he
should first go, to make his aboad. The
common course is, to go first into *France*,
and then into *Italy*, and so home by *Germany*, *Holland* and *Flanders*, as I did once:
but my opinion is, that 'tis better for a
Young Man to go first into *Italy*, and returning by *Germany*, *Holland* and *Flanders*,
come into *France*, to give himself there
the last hand in breeding. And my reason

son is this; For seeing the intention of Travelling, is to make a Man a wise Man, not a finical Man, it's better to season his mind betimes with a staid wise Breeding, than to fill it up to the brim at first with a phantastical giddiness, which having once gotten possession of the mind, bolts the doors on the inside, locks out all forms of settled Reasoning, and makes my young man delight in nothing but Vanity, Cloths, Dancing, Liveries, Balls, and such meer outsides: I would therefore have my young Nobleman's *Governour* to carry him immediately into *Italy* at fifteen or sixteen; and there season his mind with the gravity and wise maximes of that Nation, which hath civilized the whole world, and taught mankind what it is to be a Man. Having spent two or three years in *Italy* in learning the Language, viewing the several Courts, studying their Maxims, imitating their Gentile Conversation, and following the sweet Exercises of Musick, Painting, Architecture, and Mathematicks, he will at his return know what true use to make of *France*. And having spent three years more there, Learning Fence, Dance, Ride, Vault, Handle his Pike, Musket, Colours, &c. the Map, History, and Books of Policy; he will be ready to come home at twenty or one and twenty, a Man most compleat both

both in Body and Mind, and fit to fill the place of his Calling.

What to learn in France, and what not. 5. I say, *Make true use of* France. For I would not have my young Traveller imitate all things he sees done in *France*, or other Foreign Countries; I would have him learn of the *French* a handsome confidence, but not an impudent boldness. He must learn of them to come into a Room with a *Bonne mine*; but not to rush into a Mans Chamber, as they do, without so much as knocking at the Door. He must learn of them to dance well, to get a good Grace in walking and saluting, as they do; but he must not dance as he walks as many of them do. He must learn of the *French*, to become any Clothes well; but he must not follow them in all their Phantastical and fanfaron Clothings. He must learn to fence well, as they do; but I would have his Sword stick faster in the scabbard than theirs usually do. In fine, I would have him open, airy, and gallant as they are; but not affecting to be the Gallants of all Ladies, as they do.

What in Italy, and what not. So in *Italy*, I would have him learn to make a fine House; but I would not have him learn of the *Italians* to keep a good House. He may learn of them to be Sober and Wise; but I would not have him learn of them to be jealous and distrustful. I would have him learn of the *Italians*,

to

to receive those that visit him with great Civility and Respect; but I would not have him stand upon all their little Forms and incommodious Punctilio's: I would have him to be free of his Hat, as they are, but I would have the Heart to go to the Hat as well as the Hand, and his inclination to be concern'd in the Compleǌment.

In *Germany*, I would have him learn to offer a Man a Cup of Wine at his coming in; but I would not have him press so much Wine upon him, as he shall not be able to go out again, as they often do. I would have him learn of them to go freely to War for the defence of his Country; but I would not have him learn the custom of those vendible souls there, who carry their lives to Market, and serve any Prince for Money. I like well their shaking hands with you, when you first enter into their houses; but I like not their quarrelling with you for not pledging a health of a yard long, which would ruin yours. I like very much their singular modesty and chastity, which allows not bastards to be free men of the most ordinary trades; but I like not their endless drinking in feasts, which is able to make them freemen of all vices.

What in Germany and what not.

In *Holland* also I would have him learn to keep his house and hearth neat; but I would not have him adore his house, and stand in such awe of his hearth, as not to dare to make a fire in it, as they do. I would have him learn of them a spare diet; but I would not have him drink so much, as would keep him both in good diet and cloths, as they do. I would have him learn of them their great Industry and Oeconomy; but not their rude exacting upon Noblemen Strangers in their Inns, for their Qualities sake only, as they do. I would have him learn of them a singular love to his Country; but he must take heed of their clownish hatred of Nobility. Thus in all Countries I would have my young Traveller do, as men do at a great Feast, where there is no fear of starving; that is, not eat greedily of all that's before him, but fall to the best Meats, and leave the worst for the Waiters.

6. That he may follow the foresaid Rule the better, and pick out of every Country what's the best in it, let his Governour lead him betimes into the best Company, for there the best Lessons are to be learned. Now by the word *best*, I do not mean the greatest Men in Birth, but in parts. For the world is not so happy, as that the greatest Men are always the

the best : but by the word, *best*, I mean those that are the wisest, the best bred, the best principled, the best behaved, and the most cryed up by civil Persons : for of such Men much is to be learned : Their life is a perpetual Lecture ; their words so many Oracles ; their discourses so many wise Maxims : and though young Men be not able to bring their dish with them, and club wit equally with these Men, yet it's a great matter to sit still in their Company, and be a respectful *Catechumen* to them. For if it be true which *Quintilian* saith of those that love *Cicero*, *Ciceronem amasse, profecisse est*, it's also most certain, that a Man that loves good Company, must be good himself in time.

7. And that he may be able to appear in good Company without blushing, his Governour must get him, as soon as he can, to speak the Language of the place in handsome terms, and with a good accent. Next he must have a care that he be well adjusted and set out in apparel : For if anciently Jewels were called the Ushers of Ladies, because all Doors flew open to them that presented themselves so richly adorned ; so now a-days good Clothes may be called Mens Ushers, seeing they make way for them into all Companies. He must have a care that he know his Congies perfectly, and have a free Garb or

Car-

Carriage, a Cavalier way of entering into a Room; a gratefull managing of his mouth and smiles; a chironomy or decent acting with his hands, which may humor his words gravely and freely, yet not affectedly or mimically: In fine, a liberty or freedom in all his actions, which the *French* call *liberté du corps*; and it must appear to be *à la negligence*, and yet must be perfectly studied aforehand. And though these things be but the *Elements* and *Alphabet* of breeding, yet without them he can never spell Gentleman rightly, though his inside be never so good. Indeed it's long ago that great Men dwelt no more in thatched Houses.

8. But it is not enough to get him into Language and Garbs, if he get him not into Coach and Liveries, without which he can never appear at Court, or in good Company, especially in *Rome* and *Paris*, the two chief Towns of long abode abroad. For let a man be of a Race as ancient Plutarch. as the *Autocthenes* of *Athens*; who said they were as ancient as the Earth; and let him quarter his coat of Arms with the three *Lyons* of *England*, and the three *Flower-de-lys* of *France*, as I know a Gentleman of *Little Britany* doth, (by the grant anciently of both those Kings) yet I dare boldly say this, that in *Paris* no colours blazon a Mans nobility behind his Coach so much

as

as three Lacqueys and a Page, in a handsome Livery. In other Towns of *France*, where young Gentlemen used to live at first, till they get the Language, a couple of saddle horses would be very useful, both to take the air on, as also to visit the Gentry in the Country at their Summer Houses, where a Man will find great Civilities and Divertisements. Besides, riding out so in the fresh evenings of Summer, will not only wean my young Gentleman from little Company, and the crowd of his Countrymen, who will be then pressing upon him; but will also afford his Governour many fine solitary occasions of plying him alone with good Counsels and Instructions.

9. And seeing I have touched something before of his Servants and Lacqueys, I will add this, That seeing it is none of the least blessings of a young Gentleman to have good Servants about him, it belongs to his Governour, not only to choose him good ones, but also to have power to turn away bad ones. Many Men carry over with them *English* Servants, because they were their School-fellows, or their Tenants Sons; and these are of little use for a long time, and even then when a Man hath most need of Servants. Besides, they are often too familiar with their Masters, their old Play-fellows; and as often trouble-

troublesome to their *Governors* by taking their young Masters part against them; and by ravelling out at night, as they get their Masters to bed, all that the prudent Governor hath been working in the day time. Others carry over Frenchmen with them: but these often, by reason of their prerogative of Language, which their Masters want at first, get such an ascendent over them, that they come often-times to be bold and sawcy with them. For my part, I would have his Governor to take him new Servants in every place he comes to stay; and those sightly, rather than too sprightly Youths: Dull people are made to tug at the Oar of Obedience, saith *Aristotle*, whilst witty People are fitter to sit at the Helm of Command.

But then, a Governor ought to take good security that such Servants become faithfull, and impose not on his Master, or betray him in any thing to his Countrymen, amongst whom he is a stranger: For, Travellers above all others find it true, that *Frons nulla Fide*.

10. But I am to blame to give advice to Governors whom I suppose to be wiser Men than my self; and therefore will end here, by willing them a good journey and safe return: To the effecting of both which I found no better Secret, than that in my last journey, which was to be mounted upon our own Horses (five of us together) and to spare for no cost: For by this means we went at our own rates, and eat to our own minds: so true is the Italian Proverb, *Picole giornate grandi spese, ti conducano sano al tuo paese*.

In fine, I would have my young Traveller make the same prayer to God, as *Apollonius Thyaneus* made to the Sun at his going out to Travel, that is, That he would be so favourable to him, as to shew him all the bravest and best Men in the World.

A VOYAGE TO ITALY.

PART I.

BEfore I come to a particular description of *Italy*, as I found it in my Five several Voyages through it, I think it not amiss to speak something in general of the Country it self, its Inhabitants, their Humours, Manners, Customs, Riches, and Religion.

For the Country it self, it seemed to me to be *The Fertility* Nature's *Darling*, and the *Eldest Sister* of all other *of Italy.* Countries ; carrying away from them all the greatest blessings and favours, and receiving

such

such gracious looks from the *Sun* and *Heaven*, that if there be any fault in *Italy*, it is, that her Mother *Nature* hath indulged her even to wantonness: Witness luxuriant *Lombardy* and *Campania* antonomastically *Fælix*, which *Florus*, *Trogus*, and *Livy*, think to be the best parts of the World, where *Ceres* and *Bacchus* are at a perpetual strife, whether of them shall court Man the most; she by filling his Barns with Corn, he by making his Cellars swim with Wine: Whilst the other parts of *Italy* are sweating out whole *Forests of Olive-Trees*, whole *Woods of Lemons* and *Oranges*, whole *Fields* of *Rice*, *Turky Wheat*, and *Muskmillions*; and where those bare Hills, which seem to have been shaven by the Sun, and to have cursed *Nature* for their Barrenness, are oftentimes impregnated with *Marbles*, that become the Ornaments of Churches and Palaces, and the Revenues of *Princes*: witness the *Prince* of *Massa*, whose great Riches are his Marble Quarries: *Nature* here thinking it a far more noble thing to feed Princes, than to feed Sheep. It abounds also in Silk-worms, out of which they draw great Profit: And for the support of these little Republicks, one may see with what care they nurse innumerable Groves of Mulbery-Trees, on whose leaves they feed. The curious Work that is made by those Worms, is none of the least of the Wonders of Nature; which tho an Excrement of theirs, yet serving oftentimes to our Pride, as well as to our necessary use; and in both for our Apparel: It may be said of us, that our Clothing is still like that of our first Parents; or at least but one

remove

Part I. A Voyage to ITALY.

remove from Leaves. It's rich alſo in *Paſtu-rage* and *Cattle*, eſpecially in *Lombardy*, where I have ſeen Cheeſes of an exceſſive greatneſs, and of a Parmeſan goodneſs. The ſurface alſo of the Earth is covered with many curious *Simples* and wholeſome *Herbs* : Hence ſo many rare Eſſences, Cordials, Perfumes, Sweet Water, and other Odoriferous Diſtillations, ſo common here, that Ordinary Barbers and Laundreſſes will ſprinkle them in your Face, and perfume your Linnen with them over and above your bargain. Hence none of the meaneſt to be ſeen in *Italy*, are the *Fondaries* or Stilling-Houſes of the *Great Duke* of *Florence*, the *Speciary* or Apothecaries Shops of the *Dominicans* of *St. Marco*, and of the *Auguſtins* of *St. Spirito* in *Florence*; of the *Roman College*, and of the *Mmimes* of *Trinita de Monte* in *Rome* : where even death it ſelf would find a cure in *Nature*, had not her great Creator otherwiſe determimined, when by the Sin of mankind, he was provoked to pronounce a Curſe on Nature's ſelf. In fine, it excels in all kind of Proviſions either for dyet or ſport ; and I have ſeen in *Rome* whole cartloads of Wild Boars and Veniſon brought in at once to be ſold in the Market; and above threeſcore Hares in *Florence* brought in, in one day, by the two Companies of Hunters, the *Piacevoli* and *Piatelli*, on a general Hunting day.

Yet after all this, ſome cry out againſt *Italy*, for being too hot ; and paint us out its Air as an unwholeſom Peſtilential Air ; its Sun, as an angry Comet, whoſe beams are all pointed with Plagues and Fevers, and the Country it ſelf

An Objection againſt Italy.

4   A Voyage to ITALY.   Part I.

self, as a place where starving is the only way to live in health, where Men eat by Method and Art; where you must carry your body steadily, or else spill your life; and where there are so many Provincial Sicknesses and Diseases; as the *Catarrhs* of *Genoa*, the *Gout* of *Milan*, the *Hemerrhoids* of *Venice*, the *Falling Sickness* of *Florence*, the *Fevers* of *Rome*, and the *Goistre* of *Piedmont*.

Answer.

Baltazar Bonifacius lib. bil. Iudic. s l. 13. c. 13.

For my part, when I am told, that there were in *Pliny*'s time, fourteen millions of Men in *Italy*: when I read that there are now above three thousand Cities in *Italy*, and most of them Cities of *Garbo*: when I meet with National Diseases in every other Country, as the *Kings-Evil* in *Spain*, the *Pox* in *France*, the *Consumption* in *Portugal*, the *Colick* in *England*, the *Dysentery* in *Gascony*, the *Head-ach* in *Tolouse, &c.* when I reflect how this *Sun* hath blessed *Lombardy*, and made *Campania* Happy: when I call to mind, that it hath filled the Cellars of *Italy* with above Thirty several sorts of Wines: when I remember what Health it hath poured into several Herbs here, what admirable Fruits it furnisheth the Markets withal, what Ornaments it affords to God's Houses, crusting almost all the chief Churches of *Italy* with fair marbles: when I consider, in fine, how this *Sun* hath helpt to make so many brave Soldiers and Scholars, I dare not speak ill of the *Sun* or *Air* of *Italy*, lest *Balzac* check me, as *Gracchus* did him, who spoke ill of his Mother, with a *Tu Marri mee maledicis, quæ Tiberium Gracchum genuit? Darist thou speak ill of that Sun which helps to make Cæsar?*

Sol & homo generant hominem.

Plutarchus in Gracc[h]o siz :c. in 2. vol. Liter.

If

Part I. **A Voyage to ITALY.**

If this great blessing of *God*, *this warm Sun*, which hath so throughly baked the *Italian Wits*, that while (according to the observation of *Charles* the *V*.) the *French* appear not wise, but are wise; the *Spaniards* appear wise, but are not wise; the *Dutch* neither appear wise, nor are wise. Hence the *Italians* anciently afforded us those prodigies of Wit and Learning, and set' us those fair Copies in Liberal Arts and Sciences,' which all men would follow, but none attain to so much as the *Italians* themselves.

The Italians bless and their Wits.

In fine, it cannot be said that any Country in the world did ever produce so many learned Men and Heroes as this: For 'twas here that the renowned Philosophers *Pliny*, *Cato* and *Seneca* flourished, as well as the famous Orators *Cicero*, *Hortensius*, *Porcius*, *Latro*, *Ginius*, *Gallio*, *Milius*, *Fuscus*, and *Antonius*; the great Historians *Livy*, *Tacitus*, *Valerius Maximus*, *Salust*; the delicate Poets, *Virgil*, *Lucretius*, *Ovid*, *Catullus*, *Tibullus* and *Propertius*: The fam'd Satyrists, *Horace*, *Juvenal* and *Persius*: The noble Comedians *Plautus* and *Terence*; with infinite others. In the last Ages, she blest mankind with those great Divines *Tho. Aquinas*, *Bellarmin* and *Baronius*; and taught us to know the harmony of her Language, by the sweetness of the Oratory of the learned *Pansarolus*, *Manutii*, *Varchi* and *Loredano* : The Historians, that made themselves to be taken notice of as excellent Persons and learned Men, were *Guicciardine*, *Bentivoglio*, *Davila* and *Strada*. *Picus Mirandula*, *Volaterranus* and *Rudolphus* gave Rules of Humanity to her improving and ambitious

bitious Youth: *Ficinus* and *Cardan* became her Philosophers; *Tasso, Sanazarius Marino, Petrarch* and *Guarini* were her Poets: And for Architects and Statuaries she boasts *Brunallefchi, Palladio, Fontana: Oliverio* and *Bernini* have been excellent in Sculpture: and, to name no more, *Raphael, Michael Angelo, Titian* and *Sarto* were her excellent Painters. If it be said, that there is at present a decay of Learning amongst the *Italians*, it cannot be wholly denyed; but then one may as freely enquire, whether it be not only when they stand at the feet of their Noble Ancestors; not as they are compared with any other parts of the learned World. However it be as to other things; for other Languages besides their own, the people of *Italy* are generally great strangers to 'em; the Latin it self not excepted. I might proceed and write a Volume of her noble valiant Heroes, who for long Series of Years upheld the Grandeur of Old *Rome*; but I must remember that I am a Traveller, no Historian. It will therefore be sufficient for me to say, that she had never been saluted with the Title of Mistress of the World, had she not nursed up in her Bosom such great Men.

Antient & modern Captains.

And if the antient *Italians* had their brave Captains, their *Scipio, Duilius, Marius* and *Cæsar*, the Modern *Italians* have their *Scipio* too, to wit, their *Alexander Farnese*, whose true actions make Hero's in *Romances* blush, having done that really which Fables can scarce feign in Gallantry, their *Duilius* too, their *Andrea Doria* the *Neptune* of the *Ligurian Seas*, who alone taught his Country not to serve; their *Marius* also, to wit,

their

their brave *Caftruccio*, who from a Common Souldier mounted up by deferts to the highest Military Commands in the Emperor's Army. In fine, their *Cæfar* too, to wit, the *Marquifs Spinola*, or rather the *Achilles* of *Italy*, who took that other *Troy*, *Oftend*, after three years fiege: this Siege was far more famous than that of *Troy*, becaufe far truer. For in the Siege of *Troy* it was *Poetry* only that made the War, that framed and filled the *Wooden Horfe* with Worthies; that dragged *Hector* round about the Walls; it was Pen and Ink that killed fo many Men *fomno vinoque fepultos*; and *Troy* was eafily burnt, becaufe it was built of *Poets Paper*. But at *Oftend* all was real, and all *Europe* almoft, who had their forces or eyes there, were witneffes of it; and all this done by *Spinola* an *Italian*.

See Verfte Reftitution of d cay d Intelligence

Italy was governed by divers Kings, and became fubject to feveral Republicks; untill at length her cheif City *Rome* became the feat of an univerfal Empire.

She hath been called *Saturnia* from *Saturn*; *Latium*, *Oenotria*, and *Hefperia*, from three other Princes, who planted feveral Colonies there: tho it may feem that the *Grecians* had given her this name becaufe of her wefterly fituation: fome affirm, that K. *Italus*, others that ןוֹתל (Oxen bred here) gave it the name of *Italy*; But thefe names were us'd for *Italy*, when it was at firft Subject to thofe Kings, the utmoft extent of whofe Dominion was not more than half of what *Italy* now is. The fucceeding Confuls fubdued the Neighbouring Nations by degrees: And the *Roman* Empire was not eftablifhed till the happy Reign of *Auguftus*: Its grandeur began

8   A Voyage to ITALY. Part I.

gan to decline in the Fifth Century, when the *Goths, Lombards, French, Normans, Saracens, Germans*, and many other Nations did in their turns revenge the Injuries that had been done them, and every one in their time settled and seated themselves in *Italy*. But the Emperor *Justinian* expel'd numbers of these Barbarians by the good Conduct and Valour of his brave Captains *Bellisarius* and *Narsus*, and erected an Exarchate in the City of *Revena*. But the *Lombards* again recovered it, and being now its Lords, founded the Kingdom of *Lombardy* A. D. 508, in *Gallia Cisalpina*. This Kingdom stood for about 204 years; but was utterly ruin'd by *Charlemain* 774, who thereupon gave to the See of *Rome* a considerable part of its Teritories. The *Moors* did, in the ninth, tenth and eleventh Centuries, make Incursions into *Italy*; and took possession of the *Island* of *Cicily*, but the *Normans* made head against 'em, and drove them out A. D. 1058. Afterwards the *French* and *Spaniard* have by turns obtained the Government: But at present all the Princes that possess land in *Italy* act at their own pleasure, and conformably to their own Interests, depending either on the Pope or the Emperor of *Germany*.

The Italian Humor.

As for the *Italian Humour*, it is a middling humour, between too much *gravity* of the *Spaniard*, and too great *levity* of the *French*. Their gravity is not without some fire, nor their levity without some flegm. They are apish enough in Carneval time, and upon their Stages as long as the Vizard is on; but that once off, they are too wise to play the Fools in their own Names, and own it with their own Faces. They have

strong

Part I. A Voyage to ITALY.

strong Fancies, and yet solid Judgments. A happy temper, which makes them great *Preachers*, *Politicians and Ingeniers*; but withal they are a little too *melancholy* and *jealous*: They are great Lovers of their Brethren and near Kindred, as the First Friends they are acquainted withal by Nature; and if any of them lie in pass and fair advancement, all the rest of his Relations will lend him their Purses, as well as their Shoulders, to help him up, though he be but their younger Brother. They are sparing in Diet, whereby they both live in health and live handsomly, making their Bellies contribute to the maintenance of their Backs, and their Kitchin help to the keeping of their Stable. Sobriety is one of their principal moral Virtues, for they neither eat nor drink to excess. It is the greatest affront for a man to be called *Imbriaco* or Drunkard; And notwithstanding all the excellent wines they have in *Italy*, one shall never see any Person drunk there. They are ambitious still of Honors, remembring they are the Successors of the Masters of the World, the Old *Romans*; and to put the World still in mind of it, they take to themselves the glorious Names of *Camillo, Scipione, Julio, Mario, Pompeo*, &c. They are as sensible also of their Honour, as desirous of Honours; and this makes them observe their Wives, even to jealousie, knowing that for one *Cornelius Tacitus*, there have been ten *Publii Cornelii*; and that *Lucius Cornificus* is the most affronting Man. They are hard to be pleased, when they have been once incensed, but they care not to take revenge in the open field.

In fine, they affect very much compounded names as *Piccolomini, Capilupo, Bentivoglio, Malespina, Boncompagno, Malvezzi Riccobono, Malatesta, Homodei*, and such like married Names.

Their manners.
See Monsignor Casa, Stephano Guazzo, Baltazar Castiglione

As for their *Manners*, they are most commendable. They have taught them in their Books, they practise them in their actions, and they have spread them abroad over all *Europe*, which owes its Civility unto the *Italians* as well as its Religion. They never affront strangers in what Habit soever they appear; and if the strangeness of the Habit draw the *Italians* eye to it, yet he will never draw in his mouth to laugh at it. As for their Apparel or Dress, it's commonly Black and Modest. They follow the *French* in fashion, but not too hastily, except in those places that are of the *Spanish* Faction, or under that Government, for then one shall see them drest as well as walk all *Spanish*.

They value no Bravery but that of *Coach* and *Horses* and *Staffers*; and they sacrifice a world of little Satisfactions to that main one of being able to keep a Coach. Their *Points de Venice, Ribbons* and *Gold Lace*, are all turned into *Horses* and *Liveries*; and that Money which we spend in Treats and Taverns, they spend in Coach and Furniture. They are indeed frugal almost to excess; for it is usual for *Princes* and *Cardinals*, that have received a Present of Sweetmeats, Fowls, &c. to make sale of 'em to the Confectioner or Poulterer, &c. which would here be thought

no

no lefs than the effects of a covetous and miferable temper.

They will abufe no one by a Satyrical Drolling or Jefting, or making fuch fevere Reflections that one is not able to bear. It is no cafie matter for a Stranger to find accefs to their company, but, once gain'd, it will be found very fweet, civil, and obliging, fo as they may neither offend the Company in which they are, nor any Perfon, Relation or Friend; fo refpectful are they one to another, that the greateft familiarity does not make them recede from all ftricteft Rules of courteous Carriage. They are moft extreamly civil to Strangers, avoiding whatfoever might difguft them; they will not take any occafion of refentment from a Stranger; from hence it is that they avoid induftrioufly to ask any one of his Religion; nor will, when know, enter into any Difputes about that Subject that may occafion a Quarrel.

They do not only fuffer every one to fpeak in his turn, but alfo attend till he has done, counting it a piece of ill breeding for any one to interrupt another in his Difcourfe: they whifper not in Company, nor talk in another Language, that all the Company does not underftand; and Backbiting is with them look'd on as an unpardonable Affront.

They are precife in point of *Ceremony* and *Reception*, and are not puzzled at all when they hear a great man is coming to vifit them. There's not a man of them, but he knows how

Their Ceremonies.

to

to entertain men of all conditions; that is, how far to meet, how to place them, how to ſtile and treat them, how to reconduct them, and how far. They are good for *Nunciatures*, *Embaſſies*, and *State Employments*, being men of good behaviour, looks, temper, and diſcretion, and never outrunning their buſineſs. They are great Lovers of *Muſick*, *Medals*, *Statues*, and *Pictures*, as things which either divert their Melancholy, or humor it: and I have read of one *Jacymo Raynero*, a Shoemaker of *Bolognia*, who gather'd together ſo many curious Medals of Gold, Silver and Braſs, as would have become the Cabinet of any Prince. In fine, they are extreamly civil to one another, not only out of an awe they ſtand in one towards another, not knowing whoſe turn it may be next to come to the higheſt Honours, but alſo out of a Natural Gravity and Civil Education, which makes even *School-boys* (an inſolent Nation any where elſe) moſt reſpectful to one another in words and deeds, treating one another with *Poſtra Signoria*, and abſtaining from all *gioco di mano*. Nay, Maſters themſelves here never beat their Servants, but remit them to Juſtice, if the fault require it; and I cannot remember to have heard in *Rome* two Women ſcold publickly, or Man and Wife quarrel in words, except once, and then they did it ſo privately and ſecretly, and ſcolded in ſuch a low tone, that I perceiv'd the *Italians* had Reaſon about them, even in the midſt of their Choler.

As

As for their *particular Customs*, they are many. They marry by their Ears oftner than by their Eyes, and scarce speak with one another till they meet before the Parish Priest, to speak the indissolvable words of *Wedlock*. They make Children to go bareheaded till they be four or five years old, hardning them thus against *Rheums* and *Catarrhs* when they shall be old. Hence few People in *Italy* go so warm on their Heads as they do in *France*, Men in their Houses wearing nothing upon their Heads but a little *Calotte*, and Women for the most part going all bareheaded in the midst of Winter it self. Women here also wash their Heads weekly in a wash made for the nonce, and dry them again in the Sun, to make their Hair yellow, a colour much in vogue here among Ladies. And one may add to this, that they paint, than which nothing is more common; and for all sorts of Ornaments and Decorations, they use as much as their Husbands and Friends will permit: There goes a Saying of 'em, That *they are Magpies at the Door, Saints in the Church, Goats in the Garden, Angels in the Streets, Syrens in the Windows, and Devils in the House.* The Men throw off their Hats, Cuffs, and Bands, as well as their Cloaks, at their return home from Visits or Business, and put on a grey Coat, without which they cannot dine or sup; and I have been invited to dinner by an *Italian*, who before dinner made his Men take off our Hats and Cloaks, and present every one of us (and we were five in all) with a colour'd Coat, and a little Cap, to dine in. At dinner they serve in the best Meats first, and eat backwards; that is, they

begin

begin with the second course, and end with boyl'd Meat and Pottage. They never present you with Salt, or Brains of any Fowl, left they may seem to reproach unto you want of Wit. They bring you Drink upon a *Sottocoppa* of Silver, with three or four Glasses upon it, two or three of which are strait-neck'd Glasses, (called there *Caraffa's*) full of several sorts of Wines or Water, and one empty drinking Glass into which you may pour what quantity of Wine and Water you please to drink, and not stand to the discretion of the waiters, as they do in other Countries. At great Feasts no man cuts for himself, but several *Carvers* cut up all the Meat at a Side-table, and give to the Waiters, to be carried to the Guests; and every one hath the very same part of Meat carried unto him, to wit, a *Wing* and a *Leg* of wild Fowl, &c. left any one take exceptions that others were better used than he. The Carvers never touch the Meat with their Hands, but only with their Knife and Fork, and great silver Spoon for the Sauce. Every man here eats with his Fork and Knife, and never toucheth any thing with his Fingers but his Bread; this keeps the Linen neat, and the Fingers sweet. If you drink to an *Italian*, he thanks you with bending, when you salute him, and lets you drink quietly, without watching (as we do in *England*) to thank you again when you have drank, and the first time he drinks after that, will be to you, in requital of your former Courtesie. They have a strange way of returning Affronts when they happen; they break, if they can, a Bottle of Ink on the person, especially if she is

a Woa Woman, or else over the Door of the House, so that it remain spotted; and this is taken for the greatest mark of Infamy that can remain upon one. It is very troublesome to travel with Fire-arms here, because we are forc'd in most Cities to leave 'em at the Gate with the Guard, till such time as we leave the place: This is done to prevent private Assaults and Murders, which would happen here very often, by reason of their Jealousie, did they not take this course. When we part from one City, we must either take a Bill of Health, or we shall not be admitted into another.

They count not the hours of the day, as we do, from *twelve* to *twelve*, but they begin their count from *Sun-set*, and the first hour after *Sun-set* is *one a-clock*; and so they count on till *four and twenty*, that is, till the next *Sun-set* again. I have often dined at sixteen a-clock, and gone abroad in the Evening, to take the Air, at two and twenty. They call Men much by their Christian Names, *Signor Pietro*, *Signor Francesco*, *Signor Jacomo*, &c. and you may live whole Years with an *Italian*, and be very well acquainted with him, without knowing him, that is, without knowing his distinctive Surname. People of quality never visit one another, but they send first to know when they may do it, without troubling him they intend to visit; by this means they never rush into one anothers Chambers without knocking, as they do in *France*; nor cross the Designs or Business of him they visit, as they do in *England*, with tedious dry Visits; nor find one another either undressed in Clothes, unprovided in Complements

Nomen, quasi nomen tamen, St. Aug.

plements and Difcourfe, or without their Attendants and Train. In the Streets Men and Women of Condition feldom or never go together in the fame Coach, except they be ftrangers, that is, of another Town or Country; nay, Husbands and Wives are feldom feen together in the fame Coach, becaufe all men do not know them to be fo. In the Streets, when two Perfons of great quality meet, as two *Ambaffadours*, or two *Cardinals*, they both ftop their Coaches, and complement one another civily, and then retire; but ftill he that is inferiour muft let the other's Coach move firft. If any man, being a foot in the Street, meet a great man, either in Coach, or a foot, he muft not falute him in going on his way, as we do in *England* and *France*, without ftopping, but he muft ftand ftill whilft the other paffeth, and bend refpectfully to him as he goes by, and then continue his march. In fine, of all the Nations I have feen, I know none that lives, clothes, eats, drinks and fpeaks fo much with Reafon as the *Italians* do.

Their Riches.
As for their *Riches*, they muft needs be great. That which is vifible in their magnificent Palaces, Churches, Monafteries, Gardens, Fountains, and rich-furnifh'd Rooms, fpeaks that to be great which is in the Coffers: and that which the King of *Spain* draws vifibly from *Naples* every year, fhews what the other parts of *Italy* could do for a need, if they were put to it by neceffity. Nay, I am of opinion, that the very *Sacrifty* of *Loretta*, the *Gallery* of the *Duke* of *Florence*, and the *Treafury* of *Venice*, would upon an emergent occafion of a *Gothick*
or

or *Turkish* Invasion, be able to maintain an Army for five years space; and the Plate in Churches and Monasteries would be able to do as much more, if the owners of it were soundly frighted with a new *Gothick* Eruption. As for the *Riches* of particular *Princes* in *Italy*, I will speak of them as I view their States here below.

The Nobles and Gentlemen of *Italy* delight to inhabit their Cities, from whence it is that they are so great, and fine, and well built, so opulent and rich, great Persons chusing more to spend their Estates in building Palaces, and adorning them with Paintings and Statues, spacious Orchards, Gardens, and Walks, and in keeping Coaches, and fine Horses, and great Retinues of Servants, &c. than in keeping great Houses and plentiful Tables. They are such Admirers of Pictures and Statues, that they will give any rate for choice Pieces of either. They love very much a Theatrical Pomp, and are seen very often at publick Shows, &c. and the inferiour Gentry affect to appear in publick with all possible splendor, chusing to deny themselves many satisfactions at home, that they may better keep a Coach, and therein make the *Tour a-la-mode* about the Streets of their Cities, as it is the manner of the Gentry to do, especially in *Venice*. When there are many Brothers of one House, 'tis not usual for more than one to marry, nor any besides the eldest, if he shall please; but if he has no Inclination, then any other, as it can be agreed on among them; and all the rest do what they can to make him great that is married; thereby to keep up the Port of the Family: But the Brothers that marry not, many of them keep and careſs themſelves in the wanton Embraces of lewd Courteſans.

There are Hoſpitals in many of their Cities, where Pilgrims and poor Travellers are entertained, and have Diet and Lodging given them for three days, beſides, a piece of Money at their departure; but we were told by ſome, that this Charity is very much abuſed of late, tho', having no occaſion to make tryal, I could not find out any means of gaining certain information. There are alſo ſome Hoſpitals to receive Children that are expos'd, where care is taken of 'em: this is ſaid to be done on purpoſe to prevent Peoples murdering their Children to conceal their Shame.

A Fleſh-dinner in *Italy* ſhall be dreſs'd till one may ſhake it to pieces upon a Fork: it is naturally more lean and dry than ours, but by their over-roaſting, &c. they leave in it no Juice at all; and their Fires are made under the Spit, that the Fat may drop on them, and give the Meat a tincture. They ſcrape Cheeſe upon all their Diſhes, even of Fleſh, counting that it gives the Meat a good reliſh. Froggs ſerv'd up is a great Diſh with them; they are uſually fry'd, and ſent up with Oyl; but at *Venice* they eat only the Loins and hind Legs; as alſo at *Florence*, and that on Fiſh-days. Snails boil'd and ſerv'd up, with Oyl and Pepper put into their Shells, is very common, and in good eſteem with them. They eat all manner of ſmall Birds, as *Wrens, Titmouſe*, &c. and many other great ones; which the *Engliſh* ne-

ver

ver feed on, as *Magpies*, *Jays*, *Woodpeckers*, *Jackdaws*, &c. and even in *Rome* 'tis common to see *Kites* and *Hawks* lying on Poulterers Stalls. They have many excellent Fruits, which come to a greater perfection than ours. They esteem very much of *Chesnuts* roasted, and the Kernels serv'd up with Juice of Lemons and Sugar: Roasted *Chesnuts* are a great part of the Diet of the poor Pesants in *Italy*. In their second Courses they frequently serve up *Pine kernels*. They often use *Water-melons*; and, at the time of the Year, *green Almonds*. They prize extreamly a kind of Sweetmeat or Confection made of Mustard and Sugar, which they call *Italian Mustard*; they use it to cool and refresh themselves. And for their Wines they use Snow, or Ice, which they keep all Summer; they that are much us'd to this way will not in this Country, even in Winter, drink without Snow.

I could not observe any Vice which the *Italians* had been guilty of so much as these; they are most extravagant in their Revenge, never forgiving any Injury; most secret and treacherous in the Design, making no discovery of the least Displeasure, till they find an Opportunity to assault; and if then prevented by some unexpected Accident, at the same time implacable in their Hatred, resolving to execute their design even in the very moment when they say they will forgive, and at that instant when they promise Pardon; whence it is that they so prophanely say, That *Vengeance is so sweet a thing, that the Almighty reserves it to himself, because he will have no Mortal partake, with him in so great a Good.* I took notice of their Lust also, which I observ'd to rage amongst them both naturally and unnaturally. Their extraordinary Jealousie I believe to be an unhappy Effect of the former, by reason of which I took notice that their Women for the most part live miserably. Add to these, that they are great Swearers, Priests and Monks themselves being scarce able to abstain from it.

The Language which they speak is a corrupt Latin, the *Goths*, *Vandals*, *Lombards*, and many other Nations, having mix'd with 'em, and taught 'em their several harsh and unpleasant Jargons; the most polite manner of expression is used chiefly at *Tuscany*; but this Dialect ought to be pronounced by a *Roman*, who sets it off with the most delicate accent, which gave occasion to that Proverb among this People, *Lingua Toscana in Bocca Romana*. Indeed the *Italian* is a very elegant Language, and deserves well to be studied by an ingenious Linguist; it is reckon'd the most harmonious and sonorious of all modern Languages, and the fittest for Songs; it is not spoken in all *Italy*, for, in *Savoy* and *Piedmont* the French Tongue is most used. In fine,

The Religion of this Country is that which we call *Roman Catholick*, or the Religion of the Papists, which they derive from *Papa*, and it signifies *Father*; the Title of the universal Pontif, tho' they do generally assume to themselves the name of *Catholicks*, how notorious soever it be, that there are Churches in the World, and those not a few, that have like Pretensions to be of the Church Catholick, who yet are not

of

of her Communion. Their Religion is professed all over *Italy*, and the Inquisition is in most places so strict, that it is very dangerous to be of any other, for only some few Jews are tolerated, on the account of Trade: however, in the Valleys of *Piedmont* there are many *Protestants* that are called *Vaudois's*, in number about Fifteen thousand, which have maintain'd the Purity of their Religion more than Twelve hundred years, tho' they have suffer'd very great Persecutions most part of the time by the Dukes of *Savoy*; they have lately obtain'd Liberty for the exercise of their Religion, from the present Duke.

Having said thus much of *Italy* in general, I will now come to a particular Description of it, according to the ocular Observations I made of it in five several Voyages through it; in which description, if I be a little prolix, it is because I rid not post through *Italy* when I saw it; nor will I write post through it in describing it; being assur'd that Epitomes in Geography are as dissatisfactory as Laconick Letters would be in State Relations; and that the great *Atlas*, in nine great volumes *in folio*, is not only *Atlas major*, but also *Atlas melius*.

A Voyage to ITALY. Part I.

The several Ways by which a Man may go into Italy.

THE ordinary ways which an English-man may take in going into *Italy* are five, to wit, either through *Flanders* and *Germany*, and so to fall in at *Trent* or *Trevifo*, and so to *Venice*. Or else by *France*, and so to *Marseilles*, and thence to *Genoa* by Sea. Or else by Land from *Lyons*, through *Swifferland*, the *Grifons* Country, and the *Valtoline*, and so pop up at *Brescia*. Or else from *Lyons* again through the *Valefians* Country over *Mount Sampion*, the *Lake major*, and so to *Milan*. Or else, in fine, from *Lyons* still over *Mount Cenis*, and so to *Turin*, the nearest Post-way. I have gone or come all these ways, in my five Voyages into *Italy*, and tho' I prefer the last for speed and conveniency, yet I will describe the others too, that my young Traveller may know how to steer his course, either in time of Plague or War.

My First Voyage into Italy.

MY first Voyage was through *Flanders* and *Germany*, and so to *Trent*. The way is, from *England* to *Dunkirk*; from thence to *Furnes, Newport, Ostend, Bruges, Ghent, Bruffels, Lovain, Liege, Cologn, Mayence, Francford*, and so crossing to *Munichen*, the Court of the Duke of *Bavaria*, and from thence to *Ausburg*, and *Infpruck*, you come soon to *Trent*, which stands

up-

upon the Confines of *Germany*, and lets you into *Italy*, by *Trevifo*, belonging to the *Venetians*. To defcribe all thefe 'forefaid places, would take me too much time from my defign of defcribing *Italy*, and therefore I content my felf only to have named them.

My fecond Voyage.

MY *fecond Voyage* was by the way of *France*, where I ſtarted from *Paris*, and made towards *Lyons* ; in the way I took notice of thefe places.

Iſſone a neat houfe belonging then to *Monfieur Iſſon*. *Eſſolin*. The Houfe is fo pretty, that I think it worth the Travellers feeing, and my defcribing. It ſtands in the ſhade of a thick grove of Trees, and is wholly built and furnifhed *al-Italiana*. Under the fide of the Houfe, runs a little Brook, which being received into a Baſon of Free-ſtone, juſt as long as the Houfe, and made like a Ship, (that is, ſharp at both ends and wide in the middle) it is cloven, and divided into two by the ſharp end of this Ship, and conveyed in cloſe Channels of Free-ſtone, on both ſides of the Ship or Baſon, into which it empties it felf by feveral Tunnels, or Pipes: fo that all this Water fpouting into the open Ship on both ſides, by four and twenty Tunnels, makes under the Windows of the Houſe, fuch a perpetual purling of Water, (like many Fountains) that the gentle noife is able to make the moſt jealous Man ſleep profoundly. At the other end of the Houfe, this Water iſſueth out of the other end of the faid Ship, and

is courteoufly entreated by feveral hidden pipes
of Lead, to walk into the Houfe, inftead of
running by fo faft: which it doth, and is prefently led into the Cellars, and Buttery; and
not only into thefe, but alfo into the Kitchin,
Stables, Chambers, and Bathing Room, all
which it furnifheth with Water either for
Neceffity or Pleafure. Then being led into the
curious Garden, it's met there by a world of
little open Channels of Free-ftone, built like
Knots of Flowers; all which it fills brimful,
and makes even Flowers of Water. Then running up and down here and there among the
fragrant Delights of this Garden, as if it had
forgotten its Errant to the Sea, it feems to be
fo taken with thofe fweet Beds of Flowers, and
fo defirous of refting upon them, after fo many
miles running, that it offers to turn it felf into
any pofture, rather than be turned out of this
fweet place.

Fountain-bleau. From *Iffone* I came to *Fountain-bleau*, where
I faw that Kingly Houfe, the *Nonfuch* of *France*.
It ftands in the midft of a great *Foreft* full of
The Court Royal Game, and a place of Delight of *Henry*
of th Che- the *Fourth*. The Houfe is capable of lodging
val Blanc. four Kings with feveral *Courts*. The Court of
Cheval Blanc is a noble fquare of Buildings: but
the lownefs of the Buildings and Lodgings fhews,
they are for the lower fort of People, and the
Servants-Lodgings to the Royal *Apartments*.
The Oval The *Oval Court* is a good old Building. The
Court. Kings and Queens Lodgings with their *Cabinets*
The Galle- groan under their rich gilt Roofs. The *Gallery*
ry of of *Stagge Heads* is a ftately Room; than which
Stages nothing can be more Cavalierly furnifhed;
Heads.
except

except such another *Gallery* hung with *Turkish Standards* won in War. The other long *Galleries* of *Romances* and *Fables*, painted by *Simon Voyet* and others, are much esteemed: the only pity is that such true painting should not have been employed upon true Histories. *The Galleries of Romances.*

The *Salle* of *the Conference* is a stately Room, where the Bishop of *Evreux* (afterwards called the *Cardinal du Perron*) in presence of King *Henry* the Fourth, the Chancellor, five Judges of both *Religions*, and the whole Room full of learned Men, disputed with *Monsieur Plessis Mornay*, the *Achilles* of those of *Charenton*. The Hall of *Masks*, and the Lodgings of *Madam Gabrielle* with her *Picture* over the *Chimney* like a *Diana* Hunting, are fine Rooms: yet the fair Picture cannot hinder Men from blaming her foul Life; nor from censuring that *Solœcism* of the Painter, who made Chaste *Diana* look like *Madam Gabrielle*. There are also here two Chapels, the old and the new. The old one is a poor thing; and seems to have been built for Hunters: but the new one is both neat and stately, and built upon this occasion, as a Bishop in *France* told me. A *Spanish Embassador* residing in *Paris* in *Henry* the IV. his time; went one day from *Paris* to *Fontain-bleau*, to this *French Escurial*. Arriving, he lighted after his Country fashion, at the Chappel Door (the old Chappel) and entering in, to thank God for his safe arrival, he wondred to see so poor and dark a Chapel, and asking with indignation, whether this were the *Casa di Dios*, the House of God? he turned presently away with scorn, saying, *No quiero ver mas*; I care for *The Salle of the Conference. See the publick Acts of this Conference printed An. 1603. Madame Gabriell's Picture. The Chapels.*

see-

seeing no more: not staying to see that place, where the King had so fine a House, and God so poor a *Chapel*. This being told the last King *Lewis* the XIII. he commanded forthwith the new *Chapel* to be built in that sumptuous posture we now see it.

Going out of the House, you find a handsome *Mail*, and rare *Ponds* of Water, which even baptize this place with the name of *Fountain-bleau*. In these *Ponds*, as also in the Moat about the House, are kept excellent *Carps*; some whereof were said to be an hundred years old; which, though we were not bound to believe, might make Men believe that there are *gray scales*, as well as *gray hairs*; and decayed Fishes, as well as decrepit Men: especially when *Columella* speaks of a Fish of his acquaintance, in *Cæsars* Fish-ponds near *Pansilippus*, which had lived threescore years; and *Gesnerus* relates, that in a Fish-Pond near *Haylprum* in *Suabie*, a Fish was catched *Anno* 1497, with a Brass Ring at his Gills, in which were engraven these words: *I am the first Fish which Frederick the second, Governour of the world, put into this Pond the 5 of October 1203.* By which it appears, that this Fish had lived two hundred and sixty odd years. But to return again to our Carps of *Fountain-bleau*. It's an ordinary divertisement here, to throw a half-penny loaf into the Moat among the Carps, and to see how some will mumble and jumble it to and fro; how others will puff and snuff, how such hot Passions should be found in cold Water: but every thing that lives, will fight for that whereby it lives, its Victuals.

Ha-

Part I. A Voyage to ITALY. 27

Having seen *Fountain-bleau*, I saw one extraordinary thing in the rest of the way to *Lyons*, it was an old *Inscription* in Letters of Gold, upon a Wooden Fabrick, a mile before I came to *Montargis*, importing, that the *English* being encamped here, had been forced to raise their Siege before *Montargis*, by reason of great Rain and sudden Inundations. Some of the French Historians will have it, that it was the *Count de Dunois*, that forced the English to raise the Siege here: but I had rather believe publick Inscriptions, than private flattery: and it was more honourable for the *English* to be overcome by *God* than by *Men*. *An old Inscription concerning English Men.*

From hence I passed through *Montargis*, a neat pleasant Town; in the great *Hall* of whose *Castle* is painted the History of the *Dog* that fought a *Duel* with the *Murderer* of his *Master*; and it is not strange that the *Dog* that had put on Humanity, overcame him that had put it off, to espouse the devouring humour of a *Dog*. This is the chief Town of the *Gastinous*. *Montargis.*

From hence I went to *Briare*, where I saw the cut Channel that joyns *Loire* and *Sene* together in Traffick, whose Beds otherwise stand wide from one another in situation. *Briare. The Conjunction of Loire and Sene.*

From thence to *Cosne la Charite Pougues* famous for wholesome stinking waters: *Newres* famous for Glass Houses; *Moulins* famous for Knives and Scissors.; *La Palisse*, where they make excellent Winter-Boots ; *Roanne*, where *Loire*, begins to be navigable, and so over *Terrara* Hills to *Lyons*.

Lyons is one of the greatest and richest Towns in *France*. It stands upon the Rivers *Suone* and *Rhosne*, (*Araris* and *Rhodanus*) and in-

intercepting all the Merchandise of *Burgundy*, *Germany* and *Italy*: here you have handsom people, noble houses, great jollity, frequent balls, and much bravery; all marks of a good Town: and could it but intercept either the Parliament of *Aix* or *Grenoble*, it would be as noble as its *name*, or as its *Cathedral Chapter*, whose Dean and *Prebends* are all *Counts*, and noble of four descents. They got the Title of *Counts* thus: A great contest arising between the *Chapter* of St. *John's* Church, and the *Count de Forrests*, called *Guigo*, for some rights over the Town of *Lyons*, which they both Pretended to; at last *Anno* 1166. they came to an agreement, upon this condition, that the *Count* should leave to the *Chapter* his Country of *Forrests*; which he did; and so ever since the Dean and Prebends have been called Counts of St. *John*.

A noble Chapter.

The chief things to be seen in *Lyons* are these.

S. John's Church.

1. The great Church, or Cathedral called *John's Church*. It's the Seat of an Archbishop, who is Primate of *Gaul*. St. *Irenæus* was a great Ornament of this Church, as was also *Eucherius*. Upon Solemn Days the Canons officiate in *Miters* like Bishops. They sing here all the Office by Heart, and without Book, as also without Prick-Song Musick, Organs, or other Instruments, using only the antient plain song. The High-Altar is like those of *Italy*, that is open on all sides, with a Crucifix and two little Candlesticks upon it. I never saw any hangings in this Church, not upon the greatest days, but

venera-

venerable old Walls. The Clock here is much
cryed up for a rare piece.

2. The stately new *Town-house*, of pure
white Free-stone, able to match that of *Am-* *The Town-*
sterdam; and indeed they seemed to me to be *house.*
Twins, for I saw them both in the same
year as they were in building. The curious
Stair-Case, and *Hall* above, are the things
most worthy taking notice of, the one for its
contrivance; the other for its painting.

3. The Jesuits College and fair Library.

4. The *Carthusians* Monastery upon a high *Other Ra-*
Hill. *rities.*

5. The *Minimes* Sachristy well painted.

6. The rest of the old Aqueduct upon the
Hill.

7. The *Mail*, and the sweet place of *Belle*
Cour.

8. The Heart of St. *Francis de Sales* in the
in the Church of the Visitation in *Belle Cour*.

9. The *Charite*, where all the poor, who
are kept at work with admirable Oeconomy:
It looks like a little Town, having in it
nine Courts, all built up with lodgings for the
poor, who are about fifteen hundred, and divided into several Classes, with their several
Refrectories and Chapels.

10. The Head of St. *Bonaventure* in the *Cor-*
deliers Church.

11. The Castle of *Pierre Ancise*, built upon
a Rock.

12. *Nostre Dame de Fourier* standing upon a
high Hill, from whence you have a perfect
view of *Lyons*.

13. Last-

13. Laſtly, the rare Cabinet of *Monſieur Servier*, a moſt ingenious Gentleman; where I ſaw moſt rare experiments in *Mathematicks* and *Mechanicks*, all made by his own hand; as the Sympathetical Balls, one ſpringing up at the approach of the other, held up a pretty diſtance off: the demonſtration of a quick way how to paſs any Army over a River with one Boat, and a Wooden Bridge eaſily to be folded up upon one Cart: the *Mouſe-dial*, where a little thing, like a Mouſe, by her inſenſible motion, marks the hours of the day. The *Lizard-dial* is much like the former, only the *Mouſe* moves upon a plain Frame of Wood which hath the hours marked on it; and the *Lizard* creeps upward from hour to hour. The *Night dial*, ſhewing by a lighted Lamp ſet behind it, the hours of the night, which are painted in colours upon oyled Paper, and turn about as the time goes. The *Tortoiſe-dial*, where a piece of Cork cut like a Tortoiſe, being put into a Pewter-diſh of Water, which hath the twelve hours of the day marked upon its brims, goeth up and down the Water a while, ſeeking out the hour of the day that is then, and there fixing it ſelf without ſtirring. The Rare Engine, teaching how to throw *Granado*'s into beſieged Towns, and into any preciſe place without failing. The way how to ſet up a Watch-Tower with a Man in it, to look into a Town from without, and ſee how they are drawn up within the Town: A way how to change Dining-Rooms three or four times with their Tables, the Seats and Gueſts being by the turning of a wheel tranſported ſitting, out of one Room into another:

Part I. A Voyage to ITALY.

ther, and so into three or four more Rooms variously hung, with Tables cover'd. The *Desk-Dial*, which throws up a little Ball of Ivory without rest, and thereby marketh the hour of the day, and sheweth what a clock it is; the Dial of the *Planets*, representing the Days of the Week by several Figures of the Planets in Ivory; the *Oval Dial*, in which the Needle that marks the Hours shrinketh in, or stretcheth out it self, according as the Oval goes; the Dial shewing to every one that toucheth it his *predominant Passion*; with a world of other rare Curiosities, all made by this ingenious Gentleman.

Leaving *Lyons*, I embark'd in a Cabanne, or little cover'd Boat, and descending the rapid *Rhosne*, I came post by Water to *Vienne*, where *Vienne.* *Pontius Pilate*, banish'd hither, threw himself off a high Tower, and kill'd himself. The Cathedral of this Town is a fair Church, dedicated to God, in the honour of St. *Maurice*; there are neither Pictures nor Hangings in this Church.

From hence I went to *Tournon*, where I saw *Tournon.* a good Library in the College.

Thence to *Valence* in *Dauphine*, where Law *Valence.* is taught.

From whence I came to *Pont Saint Esprit*, *Pont S.* famous for its long Bridge of thirty three Ar- *Esprit.* ches, and for the Bones of a Gyant, which are conserved in the *Dominicans* Convent here; and from hence to *Avignon*.

Avignon is the head Town of a little Country call'd vulgarly the *Contad le Contad d' Avignon*. *Avignon.* It belongs to the Pope, having been purchas'd

by

by one of his Predeceſſors anciently of *Jane* Queen of *Naples*, and Counteſs of *Avignon*; and it ſerved for a ſafe retreat to divers Popes conſecutively, during the Troubles of *Italy*, which laſted above ſeventy years. At laſt *Italy*, and the Pope's Territories there, being clear'd by the admirable Courage and Conduct of brave Cardinal *Albornozzo*, who conquered again all the Pope's Eſtate, the Pope *Gregory* the XI. returned home again to *Rome*. Of the 'foreſaid Cardinal *Albornozzo* I cannot omit to tell one thing; That after his great Services render'd to the Pope, being envied by ſome of the Court, who had perſwaded his Holineſs to call him to an Account for the great Summs of Money he had ſpent in reducing again the whole State of the Pope unto its Obedience; he brought the next morning a Cart laden with *Chains*, *Bolts*, *Locks* and *Keys*, belonging once to thoſe Towns which he had retaken for the Pope, and placed it under the Pope's Window; then going up, one deſiring his Holineſs to draw to a Window, to ſee his Accounts the better, he open'd the Window, and ſhew'd him below, the Cart laden with *Chains*, *Bolts*, *Locks* and *Keys*, ſaying, *Holy Father*, *I ſpent all your Money in making you Maſter again of thoſe Towns whoſe Keys, Locks, Bolts and Chains you ſee in that Cart below.* At which the Pope admiring, deſired no more Account of him, who proved his Honeſty by whole Cart-loads of Services. Ever ſince that time, *Avignon* hath belong'd to the Pope, and he governeth it by a *Vice-Legate* immediately, the Pope's Nephew, *pro tempore*, being always *Legate* of this Town.

Part I.   **A Voyage to** ITALY.   33

The things I saw here were these: 1. The *Cathedral Church*, with divers Tombs of Popes in it that died here. 2. The Church of S. *Didier*, with the Tomb of *Petrus Damianus*, who follow'd the Pope hither: He was famous for his learned Works, and his known Sanctity. 3. The *Church of the Celestins*, with the Tomb and neat Chapel of *Cardinal Peter* of *Luxemburg*, a young Man of a great Family, and of a greater Sanctity. 4. The *Carthusians* Monastery in the Bourg of *Villeneuve*, where you shall see much good painting. 5. The *Dominicans* fair Convent, with the Chapel and true Picture of St. *Vincentius Ferrerius*, a holy Man of this Order. 6. The *Cordeliers* Church, famous for its wideness, and yet not supported by any Pillars: Here lies buried Madam *Laura*, render'd so famous by *Petrarch*'s Verses; not that she was a dishonest Woman, but only chosen by him to be the Poetical Mistress of his Sonnets. 7. The Church of the Fathers of the *Christian Doctrine*, with the Body, yet entire, of the Founder of their Order, *P. Cæsar de Bus*, a Man of such singular Sanctity, that Cardinal *Richlieu*, banish'd hither, whilst he was only Bishop of *Luson*, offer'd and vow'd a Silver Lamp to God at the Tomb of this holy *Beato*. 8. The fine Free-stone Walls of this Town, the admirable Bridge, many handsome Palaces, and curious Gardens. 9. The Trading of this Town, which consists much in Silk-stuffs, perfumed Gloves, Ribbons, and fine Paper. 10. The Inhabitants here, who love to go well adjusted and appear in fine Clothes.

The Rarities.

D   From

Aix.

From *Avignon* I went by Land to *Aix* in *Provence*, an University, a *Parliament Town*, and one of the neatest Towns in *France*: of the Parliament of this Town Monsieur *du Vair* was the first President, and a singular Ornament, by reason of his famous Eloquence. This Town is the Seat of an Archbishop, and is now possessed by Cardinal *Grimaldi*, who is *Archbishop* here. From hence I went to *Marseilles*.

Marseilles.

Marseilles is a very ancient Town, built 633 years before our Saviour's time, and so famous anciently for learning, that it was compared with *Athens*. It stands upon the *Mediterranean* Sea, and hath a most neat Haven and Harbour for Ships and Galleys. I stay'd here eight days to wait upon the return of two Gaileys of *Genoa*, that had brought an Embassadour from thence into *France*, and were to return within a few days. In this time I had leisure to make a little excursive Voyage to the famous place of Devotion called *La Sainte Beaume*, where S. *Mary Magdalen* lived a most penitential life in these Mountains and Desarts, even after she had been assured of her Pardon by our Saviour himself: the place it self is able to make any Man that considereth it well melt in, to some Pennance too, and sigh at least, to see how much she (a Woman) did, and how little he (a Man) doth; for *excellentissima animadvertenti, ne mediocria quidem præstare, rubori oportet esse*, saith a great Author. In *Marseilles* it self there remain some prints of her begun Pennance; but she that had been a Sinner in the City (and perchance by that occasion only) thought the *Desart* a safer place, and so shew'd her Conversion

La Sainte Beaume.
See Baronius ad An. 35. Gordon's Chronolog. Gerard of Nazareth, in a Treatise ex professo.

Val. Max. Mulier peccatrix in civitate.

fion to be true, by flying the occafions of her former Sins.

If you ask me how *Mary Magdalen* came hi- See Baron.
ther, I muft ask you how *Jofeph* of *Arimathea* An. 35.
came into *England*; and learned *Baronius* will Genebrad
anfwer us both, by telling us, that upon a Per- Chaffonus,
fecution raifed againft the *Chriftians* in *Hieru-* and Monf.
falem, Mary Magdalen, her Sifter *Martha*, her du Vair.
Brother *Lazarus*, with *Jofeph* of *Arimathea*, and
divers others of the firft *Chriftians*, were expo-
fed to Sea in a Ship without Sails, without Rud-
der, without Anchor, without Pilot, and yet
the Ship came happily to *Marfeilles*, where *Lazarus* preaching the Faith of Chrift, was made
the firft Bifhop of this Town, and *Jofeph* of
Arimathea came into *England*.

Near to *Sainte Beaume* ftands the Town of
S. *Maximin*, famous for the Church of *S. Maxi-* S. Maxi-
min, govern'd by *Dominican* Friars. In this min.
Church are to be feen many famous *Relicks* of
S. *Mary Magdalen*, as her Head in a Cryftal
Cafe enchafed in Gold; her Body in a gilt
Chaffe, and divers other rich things.

Having feen *Marfeilles*, I embarked in the
'forefaid Gallies, and was nine days in them
before I arrived at *Genoa*, having feen in the
way *Toulon, Nice, Antibo, Monaco, Savona*,
which brought us to *Genoa*.

Thus I paffed, though tedioufly yet fecurely,
from *France* into *Italy* by Sea; and I could almoft wifh my Traveller to take the fame courfe
if he were fure to find two Galleys fo well
manned, as I did, to carry him thither; otherwife to venture himfelf (as Men ordinarily,
with extraordinary danger do) in a little *Feluca*,

D 2   a Boat

a Boat little bigger than a pair of Oars, is a thing I would wish none to do but *Pyrrhonians*, and *Indifferents*, who think danger and security to be the same thing. For my part, though I dare not say with that cowardly *Italian*, who being laughed at for his running away in a Battel, answer'd, *I was not afraid, but only had a mind to try how long a Man's Skin well kept would last:* Yet I dare say with generous *Cato*, that I repent me soundly, if ever I went by Water when I could have gone by Land.

Pyrrho dicebat, nihil interesse inter sanam & morticam.

My Third Voyage.

MY third Voyage into *Italy* was again by the way of *Paris* and *Lyons*, but now by *Geneva* and *Swisserland*.

Parting then from *Lyons*, I passed over the *Grand Credo*, a smart Hill, through *Namua* standing upon a Lake, and in two days came to *Geneva*.

Geneva is built at the bottom of *Savoy*, *France* and *Germany*.

The things which I saw in *Geneva* were these:
1. The great Church of S. *Peter*, the Cathedral anciently of the Bishop of this Town. In the Quire I saw yet remaining the Pictures of the twelve *Prophets* on one side, and the Pictures of the twelve *Apostles* on the other side, all engraven in Wood; the Pictures also of the Blessed Virgin *Mary*, and S. *Peter*, in one of the Windows. Here also I saw the Tomb of the Duke of *Bouillon*, General of the Army of *Germans*, called then in *France* the *Reiters*, who in the Battel of *Aulneau* were beaten by the Duke of *Guise*,

Geneva.

The Rarities.

Guife, and forced to fly to *Geneva*, having loft 1800 of their Men upon the place, moft of them with Charms about their Necks, which they thought would have made them fhot-free. Mounting up to the Steeple, I faw a fair *Bell* with a *Crucifix* caft upon it, and four good pieces of Ordnance, that none may fay, the *Church of* Geneva *wants Ecclefiaftical Cannons*. And a little below, in the *Belfrey*, there live in feveral Chambers three or four Families. From the top of this Church you have a fair profpect upon the Lake and neighbouring Countries; which makes them brag here, that they can fee from their Steeple into fix feveral Principalities, to wit, their own, *France, Savoy, Swiffer-land,* the *Valefians,* and the *Franchecounty :* but I told them, it would be a greater Brag to fay, that they could fee into no other Country or Dominion but their own.

2. I faw the *Arfenal*, little, but well ftored with defenfive Arms. They never forget to fhew the Ladders of the *Savoyards*, who attempted to furprize this Town by fcaling, but were themfelves taken and beheaded *a la chaude*, left fome Prince fhould have interceded for them.

3. The *Town-houfe*, with the Chamber where the Magiftrates fit in Counfel.

4. They fhew'd me here a *Library*, but none of the beft.

The Government of this Town was anciently Monarchical, and the Bifhop was Prince of it under the Duke of *Savoy*; but it is govern'd by Laymen and Minifters of *Calvin*'s way; yet the Bifhop keeps his Title ftill, and the Chapter its Revenues and Lands, which lie

lie in *Savoy*, out of the Jurisdiction of *Geneva*: Both the Bishop and Chapter have, as I was told, their Residence at *Amsy* in *Savoy*, and officiate in the Church of the *Cordeliers*. S. Francis *de Sales*, who made Four thousand Sermons to the People, was Bishop of this See.

The Lake of Swisserland, Geneva.   Having thus seen *Geneva*, I made towards *Swisserland*, leaving the Lake on my right hand, or rather taking it on my right hand, for it would needs accompany me to *Lausanna*.

This Lake is absolutely the fairest I have seen; it's fairer than either the Lake *major*, the Lake of *Como*, the Lake of *Zuric*, the Lake of *Wallinstade*, the Lake of *Isee*, the Lake of *Murat*, or the Lake of *Garda*. In some places this Lake of *Geneva* is eight miles broad, and well nigh fifty miles long. I have read of a stranger who travelling that way alone in Winter, when the Lake was all frozen over, and covered with Snow, took the Lake for a large Plain, and rid upon it eight or ten miles, to the Town, where lighting at his Inn, and commending the fine Plain, over which he had ridden, was given to understand, that he had ridden, if not in the Air, at least fifteen fathom above ground; at which the poor man, reflecting upon the danger he had been in, fell down dead with the conceit of it. Thus we are troubled not only at evils to come, but at evils past, and are never so near the danger of death, as when we are newly past it. No Animal, but Man, hath this Folly.

Lausanna.   *Lausanna* is a Town in *Swisserland*, belonging to the Canton of *Berne*. Here I saw an ancient Church of a noble Structure; and once a Bishops

shops Cathedral, but now possessed by Ministers of *Calvin*'s Communion; and the man that shewed us the Church (tho' not a *Papist*) told us, That the *Records* of that Church bore, that Mass had been said in it thirteen hundred years ago.

From *Lausanna* I went towards *Soleur*, skirting through the Cantons, sometimes of *Berne*, sometimes of *Friburg*, and sometimes in one days Journey I passed into a *Papal Canton*, and by and by into a *Protestant Canton* again, for here Papist and Protestant Villages are mingl'd together, and make the Country look like the back-side of a pair of Tables, chequer'd with white and black. In one Village you have a Cross set up, to signifie that it Is Papal, belonging to the Canton of *Friberg*; by and by, in another Village, a high Flag with the picture of a Bear in it, to signifie that it belongs to the Canton of *Berne*, and is Protestant; and yet they live civilly and neighbourly together, without quarreling about Religion.

Swisserland.

Berne signifies as much as Bear.

Passing thus along, I came to *Soleur*, (*Solaturnm* in Latin) a neat Town, and head of a Canton: they are all *Papists* here; and here it is that the *French Embassadors* to the *Swissers* alwaies reside, as the *Spanish Embassadors* do at *Lucerna*. This Town is very ancient, as the golden Letters upon the Clock testifie, for those words make *Soleur* to be only younger than Her Sister *Trevers*, which, as *Æneas Sylvius* writes, was built 1300 years before *Rome*. As for *Soleur*, I find in good Chronologers that it was built 2030 years after the Creation of the World,

Soleur.

Petrus Rimaldus in Cronolog. Trejor. ro. 1. pag. 83. in fol.

From

Murat.

From *Soleur* I went to *Murat*, a little Town famous for a great Battle fought hard by it, by the Duke of *Burgundy* and the *Swiffers*; for the Duke of *Burgundy* befieging *Murat*, the *Swiffers* came upon him with a great Army, and defeated him. I was told here, that the Duke feeing his Army defeated, and himfelf entiron'd on one fide by a Lake that is here, and on the other fide by the Enemies conquering Army, chofe rather to truft himfelf to the Lake than to his Enemies; whereupon fpurring his Horfe into the Lake, one of his Pages, to fave himfelf alfo, leaped up behind him as he took Water; the Duke out of fear either perceived him not at firft, or diffembled it till he came to the other fide of the Lake, which is two miles broad; the ftout Horfe tugged through with them both, and faved them both from drowning, but not both from death; for the Duke feeing in what danger his Page had put him, ftabbed the Page with his Dagger. Poor Prince! thou might'ft have given another Offering of Thankfgiving to God for thy efcape than this; nay, thou might'ft have been as civil as thy Horfe; thou might'ft at leaft have fav'd thy Honour, hadft thou fav'd a wretched Page, who had offended rather out of fear of Death than out of Malice; and thereby too have truly faid, thou hadft not loft all thy Men in that Battel: but Paffion is a blind thing; nothing is fo dangerous to Man as Man; and as I obferved above, we are never in greater danger than when we think our felves efcap'd. The Bones of the *Burgundians* flain in this Battel are feen in a great Chapel, which ftands a little

The Lake of Murat.

little distant from the Town, and upon the Road, with an Inscription upon it touching the time and circumstances of this Defeat.

From *Murat* I made towards *Zuric*, a head Town also of a Canton. It stands most sweetly upon a Lake, whose Crystalline Waters would delight any body else but *Swissers*. They are all here Followers of *Zwinglius*, and they tell us, when Mareschal *d'Estrée*, the *French Embassador* to *Rome*, passed that way, and lodged at the great Inn of the *Sword*, as he was combing his Head one morning in his Combing-cloth, with his Chamber-window open, some of the Townsmen, who saw him (from another opposite Window) putting on that Combing-cloth, and thinking it had been a Priest putting on the Amice, and vesting himself for to say Mass before the *Embassador* in his Chamber, began with a Dutch clamour to stir up the People to a Mutiny about the Embassador's House, and to call for the Priest that was saying of Mass: the Embassador at first, not understanding the cause of this Uproar about his House, ran down with Sword in hand, and in his Combing-cloth, to check the first Man that should dare to enter his Lodgings; but understanding at last that his Combing-cloth had caused this Jealousie, he laughed at their Folly, and retired away contented.

The best things to be seen in *Zuric* are these:

1. The neat *Arsenal*, furnish'd with store of fair Cannons and Arms of all sorts.

2. The great *Library*, but in this much less esteem'd by me, because a *Woman* had the Key

of it, and let us in to see it. This piece of false Latin at the entrance disgusted me with all that I saw there, and made me hasten out quickly: Good Libraries should not fall *en quenouille*.

3. The Wheels which draw up Water from the Lake of themselves, and empty it into several Pipes, and so convey it all over the Town.

4. The publick great *Drinking Hall*, where there are a world of little tables for Men of several Corporations or Trades to meet at, and either talk there of their Business, or make drinking their Business. Over every Table hangs the sign of each Trade; as, a *Last* for Shoemakers, a *Saddle* for Sadlers, a *Sword* for Cutlers, &c. there is a great Bell that rings to this meeting-place every day at two a clock, and when I heard so solemn a ringing, I thought it had been to some *Church-Devotion*, not to a drinking Assembly.

A long Bridge.

From *Zuric* I went by Water, that is upon the Lake, a whole days Journey, and passed under a Bridge of Wood which crossed quite over the Lake for two miles. It's entertained at the cost of the King of *Spain*, to pass the Souldiers which he often raiseth in the adjacent Countries.

Coire.

From hence I went to *Coire*, or *Cear*, the head Town of the *Grisons*; the Bishop and the Clergy of the great Church, with some few other living within the Precincts of the Cloyster of the great Church, are *Papists*, and perform their Devotions in the Church without controul; the rest of the Inhabitants are

Zwin-

Part I. A Voyage to ITALY. 43

Zuinglians, and poſſeſs the Town, yet they ſuffer the Biſhop and his Clergy to live quietly in the midſt of them. They ſhewed me here in this Church divers fine Relicks, eſpecially the Head (enchaſed in Silver) of our ancient *Britiſh* King *Lucius*, the firſt Chriſtian King that ever made profeſſion of Chriſtian Religion, and the firſt who help'd to plant it here. The ancient *Church-Office* here relates all this, as their Books ſhewed me. *S. Lucius the firſt Chriſtian King.*

From the *Griſons* I went to the Country of the *Valtaline*, a Country ſubject to the *Griſons*, and keeping its Fidelity to them, even when it would not have wanted aſſiſtance from *Spain* and *Italy*, if it would have been falſe to its Superiours the *Griſons*, under the colour of Religion; thoſe of the *Valtaline* being all *Papiſts*, and their Soveraigns the *Griſons*, *Calviniſts*. In a little Town of the *Griſons* (called *Herberga*) I was ſhew'd a Cheeſe (and given to taſt of it too) by mine Hoſt, the Mayor of the Town, a *Calviniſt* in Religion, and a venerable old man, who aſſured me ſeriouſly, that that Cheeſe was an hundred years old: a Venerable *Cheeſe* indeed. *The Valtaline.*

Between theſe two Countries of the *Griſons* and the *Valtaline* ſtands the great Hill *Berlino*, over which I paſſed, and fell from thence upon *Poſciavo*, a little Bourg, and ſo to our Ladies of *Tirano*, a neat Church, with a fair Inn hard by it. *Mount Berlino.*

Others, to avoid the Snow of *Berlino*, are forced now and then (as I was once) to paſs over the Mountain *Splug*, which is Hill enough for any Traveller. *Le Splug.*

From

Mount Aurigo.
The Lakes of Wallinflade, and Ilee.

From our Ladies of *Tirano* I went up a ſmart Hill called *Mount Aurigo*, and ſo making towards the Lake of *Wallinſtade*, I paſſed it over in a Boat, as I did alſo ſoon after that of *Iſee*, and ſo fell into the Territories of *Breſcia* in *Italy*, belonging to the State of *Venice*.

My fourth Voyage.

MY fourth Voyage into *Italy* was from *Lyons* again and *Geneva*, where I now took the Lake on my left hand, and paſſing along the skirts of *Savoy*, I came to *Boveretta*, a little Village, and ſo to St. *Maurice*, the firſt Town in the *Valeſians* Country. This Town is ſo called from St. *Maurice*, the brave Commander of the *Theban* Legion, in the primitive times, and who was martyr'd here for the profeſſion of Chriſtian Religion, together with his whole Legion. Hence an Abbey was built here by *Sigiſmund* King of *Burgundy*, and called St. *Maurice*.

S. Maurice.

The Valeſians.

Now this Country is called the Country of the *Valeſians*, from the perpetual Valley in which it lieth. The People have for their *Prince* the Biſhop of *Sion*, the chief Town of the Country: their Valley is above four days Journey long, beſides their Hills, which are two more: Moſt of their little Towns and Villages ſtand upon Hill-ſides, leaving all the plain Country for tillage and paſturage: their Houſes are low and dark, many of them having no Windows, and the reſt very little ones. *Sed caſa pugnaces Curios anguſta tegebat.* As for the People here, they are all *Papiſts*, and ſeem to be honeſt Men,

Part I.   A Voyage to ITALY.   45

Men, of stout courage, and of innocent lives, much Snow quenching their Lust, and high Mountains staving off from them all Luxury and Vice: they have short Hair on their Heads, but Beards in *folio* : they are got so far into the *grande mode*, as to wear Breeches and Doublets, but that's all, for otherwise their Clothes look as if they had been made by the *Taylors* of the old *Patriarchs*, or as if the Fashion of them had been taken out of old Hangings and Tapestry. In fine, both Men and Women here are great and massive, and not easily to be blown away; so that I may justly say of this People as Cardinal *Bentivoglio* said of the *Swissers*, that *They are good for the Alpes, and the Alpes for them*. One thing I observed particularly in this windy Country, which is, that they have many natural Fools here, which makes me think it no vulgar Error which is commonly said, that *the Climates that are most agitated with Winds produce more Fools than other Climates do*.

As for their Strength, upon a defensive occasion, they can assemble Forty thousand Men together under their known Commanders, who are oftentimes the Innkeepers, in whose Houses we lodge; but out of their own Pit they are not to be feared, having neither Spirits nor Sinews, that is, neither Ambition nor Money to carry on a foreign War. *Their Strength.*

From S. *Maurice* I went to *Martigni*, a great Inn in a poor Village, and from thence to *Sion*. *Martigni.*

Sion (anciently *Sedunum*) is the chief Town of the Country, and stands in the center of it. Here the Bishop, who is Prince, resideth with *Sion.*

his

his Chapter and Cathedral on one Hill, and his Castle stands on another Hill hard by. The Court of this Prince is not great, because of his and his Peoples quality. A good Bishop hath something else to do than to be courted, and good plain People must follow their *Trades*, not *Courts*. This Prince hath no Guards, because no Fears; and if Dangers should threaten him, his People, whose Love is his only Arsenal, have hands enough to defend him. So that the Prince and People, that is, the Body Politick of this State, and the Soul that animates it, seem'd to me like the Body natural in Man, where the Soul and the Body conspire together for their mutual Felicity.

The best Guards of a Prince.

Plus tutatur amor.

From *Sion* I went to *Lucia*, but lodged a quarter of a mile from the Town, and from thence I reached *Briga* at night.

Lucia.

Briga.

Briga is a little Village, standing at the foot of great Hills; where having rested well all night at the Colonel's House (the best *Inn* here) we began the next morning to climb the Hills for a Breakfast. For the space of three hours our Horses eased us, the ascent not being so surly as we expected from so rugged a brow of Hills; but when we came to the steep of the Hill it self, *Mount Sampion*, (one of the great Stair-cases of *Italy*) we were forced to complement our Horses, and go a foot. It was towards the very beginning of *October* when we passed that way, and therefore found that Hill in a good humour, otherwise it's froward enough. Having in one hours time crawl'd up the steep of the Hill, we had two hours more riding to the Village and Inn of *Sampion*, where

Mount Sampion.

ar-

arriving, we found little Meat, and poor Drink; cold Entertainment, tho' in a hot Season.

At laſt, having paid for a Dinner here, tho' we ſaw nothing we could eat, we were the lighter in Purſe, as well as in Body, to walk well that afternoon, rather than that after-dinner. To deſcribe you the rough way we had between *Sampion* and *Devedra*, down Hill always, or fetching about Hills upon a narrow way artificially made out of the ſide of thoſe Hills, and ſometimes ſticking out of them, as if it had been plaiſter'd to them, were able to make my Pen ake in writing it, as well as my Legs in walking it. And here I found the Proverb falſe, which ſaith, That *it's good walking with a Horſe in ones Hand*; for here we could neither ride nor lead our Horſes ſecurely, but either the one or the other were in danger of ſtumbling, that is, of falling five hundred fathom deep; for here, as well as in War, *ſemel tantum peccatur*, a Man need but ſtumble once for all his life-time: yet by letting our Horſes go looſe, with the Bridle on their Necks, and making a Man go before each Horſe, leſt they ſhould jumble one-another down, as I once ſaw the like done by Horſes in *Swiſſerland*, we arrived ſafely at *Devedra* that night. You would do well alſo to light from Horſe at the going over all the little trembling Bridges of Wood which you will find there, remembring the *Italian* Proverb, which ſaith, *Quando tu Vedi un Ponte, falli piu honore che tu non fai a un Conte*.

Devedra.

*Domodo-
fcela.*

Having repofed all night in the Houfe of the Signor *Caftellano*, we went the next Morning to *Domodofcela*, a little Garrifon Town of the State of *Milan*, troublefome enough to Travellers that pafs from *Milan* this way, and carry Piftols and Guns without Licenfe.

*Marguzzi.
Lake Major.*

From *Domodofcela* we paffed through a fine plain Country to *Marguzzi*, a little Village ftanding upon the *Lake Major*, (anciently call'd *Lacus Verbanus*) where making our bargain with our Boat-men, to carry us in one day from thence to *Sefto*, and keep aloof off from the command of all the Caftles, which now and then warn Boats to come in, and under pretence of fearching them for Merchandife, ftop Paffengers till they have fcrew'd a piece of Money out of them.

*Sefto.

Civita Caftellanza.*

Arriving fafe at *Sefto* that night, we took Coach the next day for *Milan*, and Dining at *Civita Caftellanza*, arrived betimes at that great Town which was call'd anciently *Altera Roma*, a fecond Rome.

My Fifth Voyage.

MY Fifth Voyage into *Italy* was ftill from *Lyons*, but now by the way of *Mount Cenis* and *Turin*, the ordinary Poft-road, and I think the eafieft way of all the reft.

Mount Aiguebelles.

Parting then from *Lyons* on Horfeback, we paffed through *Verpillier*, *La Tour du Pin*, *Beauvoyfin*, (whofe Bridge parts *France* and *Savoy*) and came in two days to the foot of *Mount Aiguebelles*, the Threfhold of the *Alpes*: this is a pretty breathing Hill, and may be called

a foul

Part I.   A Voyage to ITALY.   49

a foul Draught of the *Alpes*, or *the Alpes in a run-*
ning Hand, and not in that fair *Text-hand* which
I found *Mount Cenis* to be in. It hath all the Li-
neaments and Shapes of the great *Alpes*; that
is, much winding and turning, deep Precipices,
Marons, or Men with little open Chairs, to carry you up and down the Hill for a Crown, and
much stumbling work. In fine, this Hill re-
sembles *Mount Cenis*, as a proper Man may do
a Giant.

Having passed this Hill, and by it through
the very Clouds, we fell as it were out of the
Skies upon *Chambery*, the chief Town of *Savoy*, *Chambery.*
and where the Parliament resides.

We cast to be there at the solemn Entry,
which this Duke made for his new Spouse, the
third Daughter of the late Duke of *Orleans*,
when she came first into this Country. To de- *The Entry*
scribe all the *Triumphal Arches* in the Streets, *of the Duke*
with their Emblems and Motto's rarely paint- *and Du-*
ed; the stately *Throne* a little out of the Town, *chess of*
where the *Duke* and *Duchess* received the com- *Savoy.*
plements of their Subjects; the rich Liveries
of the young Townsmen on Horseback; the
Gallantry of the *Noblemen* and *Gentlemen* of the
Country (800 in all) with their Horses as fine
as they; the *Parliament-men*, and other Officers
of *Justice* all in black Velvet Gowns; the *Clergy*
and *Religious* marching in the mean time hum-
bly afoot, and in procession; the *Duke*'s two
Companies of Horse in Velvet Coats of crimson
colour, embroider'd with Gold and Silver, the
Pages and Footmen of the *Duke* and *Duchess* in
crimson Velvet laid thick with Gold and Silver
Lace! in fine, the *Duke* and *Duchess* on Horse-
    E   back,

back, as brillant as the Sun; would fill a Book alone, which I have no mind to do, seeing there is one extant already in a just Volume.

Montmeli a.

Isere.

Leaving then *Chambery* the next day after the Show, we went to *Montmelian* to dinner. This is a strong *Castle* upon a high Rock, overlooking the River *Isere*, and commanding the passage here, which is streight between the hills. The Strength of this Castle appear'd when it withstood the *Royal Army* of *Lewis* the XIII. of *France* for fifteen months, and made him raise the Siege when he had done. Here is still a strong Garrison in it, and store of Ammunition, and all things necessary for the defence of a strong place. They shew'd us in it their deep Well for fresh Water, in the midst of a high Rock; their excellent pieces of *Artillery*, one of which is said to carry four miles, that is, to Fort *Barreau*, a little Fort belonging to *France*, which is two leagues from hence, and which you see from this Castle.

Aiguebell. S. Jean Morian. Lasneburg.

From *Montmelian* we had rough way to *Aiguebelle*, thence to S. *Juan Morian*, to S. *Michel*, and at last to *Lasneburg*, which stands at the foot of *Mount Cenis*, the highest of all the Hills I passed over in my several Voyages into *Italy*, or out of it, to wit, *Sampion*, *Berlin*, *Splug*, and S. *Godarde*.

This Hill of *Mount Cenis* parting *Savoy* and *Italy*, shall be the place where I will now begin my *Description* of *Italy*, having hitherto only describ'd the several Ways into it.

Italy

Italy *described, in a Voyage thither.*

BEing arriv'd at the foot of *Mount Cenis*, anciently called *Cinisium*, and having rested all night at *Lasnebourg*, we agreed with the Marons to carry us up the Hill, and down the Hill, as also over the Plain, and in fine, all the way to *Novalese* it self. All this is to be expressed in your bargain with them, otherwise they will cavil with you, and make you go over the Plain a foot: the price is, a *Spanish Pistole* for every Man that's carried; those that are strong and vigorous ride up upon Mules, and walk down on foot.

<small>Mount Cenis.</small>

We began to mount at our going out of our Inn at *Lasnebourg*, and having passed by *La Ramassa*, (where Men are posted down the Hill upon the Snow in Sledges with great Celerity and Pleasure) after two hours tugging of our Chairmen or Marons, we came to the top of the Hill, and a little after to the *Posthouse*, and a little *Hospital* upon the Plain; thence passing by the *Chapel* of the *Transis*, (that is, of those who are found dead of cold in the Snow, and are buried here) we came to the great *Cross* and *Tavern*, where we began to descend. This Hill of *Mount Cenis* is four miles in the going up, four miles upon the plain, and two in its descent to *Novalese*.

Novalese. Arriving about noon at *Novalese*, we dined, horsed, and went that night to *Susa*.

Susa. *Susa*, anciently *Segestum*, is a strong Town, and one of the Gates of *Italy*; for this reason the *French*, in their long War with *Spain*, kept it a long time in their hands, as well as *Pignerol*, to let them into *Italy* when they pleas'd. Its Strength consists wholly in a *Castle* built upon a high Rock close to the Town, and commanding all the passage betwixt the two Mountains. This Town is famous in the latter History for the smart Action of the *French*, when they beat down the twelve several *Barriers*, whereby the Duke of *Savoy* thought to have choaked their passage: this Action is famous in History, by the name of *le pas de Suse*. Here at *Susa* begins *Piedmont*.

Le pas de Suse.
Piedmont.
S. Ambroso.
Rivolle. From *Susa* we went to S. *Ambrosio*, and passed by *Rivolle*, a fine House of the *Duke*'s, standing in a good Air, and at night we came to *Turin*.

Turin. *Turin*, anciently called *Augusta Taurinorum*, is situated in a Plain, near the foot of the Hills, and upon the Banks of the River *Po*, which begins here to be navigable, and from hence carries Boats to *Ferrara*, *Chiosa*, and *Venice*. This *Po* is a noble River, and very large in some places, especially a little below *Ferrara*; yet I have read, that in a great drouth which

Petrus a S. Romualdo, happen'd in the year of the World 2470, it *l. 16. to. 1.* was dry'd up and render'd innavigable.

This

Part I.   A Voyage to ITALY.

This *Turin* is the Seat of one of the greatest *Princes* in *Italy*, the Duke of *Savoy*, and *Prince* of *Piedmont*, who is also treated with the title of *Altezza Reale*, and *Vicario Generale del Imperio in Italia*. This House of *Savoy*, which now governs here, came anciently from *Sigismond*, King of *Saxony*, in the year of Christ 636, and hath conserved it self ever since, that is, for a thousand and odd years, in a continual series of Heroical Princes, whose Pedigree was never vitiated nor interrupted by any degenerate Offspring. Five Emperors and four Kings have issued out of this House. *The Duke of Savoy's Titles and Greatness.*

Anciently the Dukes of *Savoy* kept their Court at *Chamlery*, or else at *Bourg en Bresse*, a Country now belonging to *France*, upon exchange with the Marquisate of *Salnzzo*, as many of their tombs curiously cut in Marble in the *Augustins* Church there, yet shew. It was *Amadeo*, the fifth of that Name, Duke of *Savoy*, that transferr'd the Court to *Turin*. It was also this *Amadeo*, who in the memory of his Grandfather *Amadeo* the IV, who had defended *Rhodes* so bravely, instituted the Knighthood of the *Annunciata*, with this single Motto in the Collar of the Order, F. E. R. T. signifying, that *Fortitudo Ejus Rhodum Tenuit.*

The *Subjects* of this *Prince* are said to be about eighteen hundred thousand Souls. His whole *Country* with *Piedmont* and all, is judged to be two hundred miles long, and fifty broad. His *Forces* thirty three thousand Foot, and five thousand Horse: and his *Revennes* to be about a million of Crowns, besides what he can now and then raise out of that fat Country of *Piedmont*. *His Subjects. His Countries extent. His Forces. Revenues.*

E 3

His Interest.

mont. His *Interest* is to keep well with *France*, and not fall out with *Spain*.

The Town of Turin.

As for the Town it self of *Turin*, it's almost square, and hath four Gates in it, a strong *Cittadel* with five Bastions to it; its well furnished with good Provisions in the Market,; it stands in a fat soil, which makes it a little too dirty in Winter; and it is a University.

The things to be seen in Turin.

The chief things which I saw here, were these.

The Holy Syndon.

1. The *Domo*, or *Great Church*, in which is kept with great Devotion the *Holy Syndon*, wherein they say our Saviour's Body was wound up and buried: It's kept in a *Chapel* over the High Altar, and shown publickly upon certain days, and privatly to *Embassadors* and *Prelates* as they pass that way. The late Dutchess, Madam *Christiana*, began to make a fine *Chapel* for to keep it in, but it was not quite finished when I passed that way last. The Chapel is all of black Marble, adorned with stately black Marble Pillars: Indeed *winding Sheets* (such as this *Relick* is) are things of mourning, and are best set out in a mourning way.

Baronius Eccl. Hist. ad An. 34. num. 138.

The Cittadell.

2. The *Cittadell*, standing at the back of the Town, and keeping it in awe. This Duke and his Mother found the Convenience of this *Cittadell*, when by Factions within the Town against them, they were forced to this *Cittadell*, and there weather it out stoutly, still succour coming to them from *France*, made them Masters again of the Town, and their Enemies.

3. The

Part I.   A Voyage to ITALY.   55.

3. The Duke's new *Palace* handsomly built *The Palace* with a fair Court before it, a great *Piazza*, and a large open street leading up it. The *Chambers* are fair, and hung with hangings of Cloth of *Tyssue*, of a new and rich Fabrick, with rich embroidered Beds, Chairs, Stools, Cloth of State, and Canopies. Here you have the *Dutchesses Cabinet*, the curious *Bathing place* above, hung round with the true Pictures in Little of the prime Ladies of *Europe*. The curious invention for the Dutchess to convey her *The Bathing place* self up from her Bed-Chamber to that Bathing Room, by a Pully and a swing, with great ease and safety : the great Hall painted curiously : the Noble Stair Case : the old long Gallery 100 paces long, with the Pictures in it of the *Princes* and *Princesses* of the House of *Sa-* *The old* voy, with the Statues of the antient Emperours *Gallery.* and Philosophers in marble, with a rare Library locked up in great Cupboards : These are the chief Rooms and Ornaments of this Palace. I saw also the Apartments or Lodgings of the old Dutchess, Madam *Christiana*, which joyn to the Old Gallery, and in her Cabinet I saw many choice Pictures.

4. The New-street, which runneth from the *The New* Palace to the *Piazza Reale*, is a fair street, and *street.* built uniformly. The shops below afford great conveniency to the Towns-men, and the fair lodgings above to the Noblemen and Courtiers.

5. The *Piazza Reale* is built handsomely up *The Piazza* on Pillars, like our *Covent Garden*, and is full *Reale.* of nothing else but Noblemens Houses.

E 4   6. The

The Augustins Church.

6. The *Augustins Church*, called St. *Carlo*, standing in this *Piazza*, adorns it much, being a neat Church, and the best contrived that I saw in this Town.

The Capuchin's Church.

7. The *Capuchins Church* upon a hill out of the Town, is above the rate of *Capuchins*: but you must know who gave it, not who have it. From hence I had a perfect view of *Turin*, with the Country about it.

La Ventry Royale.

8. Some three miles out of the Town, I saw a neat House of the Dukes, called *La Ventry Royale*. The Court set round with *Staggs-Heads*; the Chambers full of good Pictures; the Hall painted with great Pictures of the Duke, his Mother, his Sisters, and other Ladies all on Horseback, as if they were going a Hunting; the Place where they keep *Phesants*, *Partridges*, and other suchlike Birds; the Stable for 100 Horse, and the neat Dogkennel, are the best things to be seen in this House.

La Valentine.

9. On the other side of the Town, about a mile off, I saw the old Dutchesses House called *La Valentine*. It stands pleasantly upon the Banks of *Po*, and is adorned with great variety of Pictures. In five or six Rooms, on the right hand of the House, they shewed me a world of Pictures of all sorts of Flowers: on the left hand as many of all sorts of Birds, with other Pictures curiously painted. The four Pictures representing the four Elements, with all that belongs to them; as, all the Birds that fly in the *Air*; all the *Beasts* that are found upon the *Earth*; all the *fishes* and *shells*, that are found in the *Water*; and all things that belong to *Fire*, are so curiously painted in their several particular

Part I. **A Voyage to ITALY.** 57

cular shapes and colours, that these four Pieces are an abridgment of all Nature, and the admiration of all that behold them. There are some other good pieces here too; as, the *Magdalen* fallen into an extasie; the *Rape* of the *Sabins*, and divers others.

The other Houses about the Town, as *Millefleur*, belonging to the Duke; the *Villa* of the Princess *Mary*; with divers others which shew themselves upon the Hill side, are very stately, and worth seeing.

Having thus seen *Turin*, we left the ordinary Road which leads to *Milan*, to wit, by the way of *Vercelle* and *Novara*, two strong towns, frontier to one another, through which I passed in another Voyage, and to avoid two Armies which lay in the way, chose to steer towards *Genoa* by the low way of *Savona*; and passing through a melancholy Country, by *Altare* and other little towns for the space of three days, we came at last to *Savona*. *From Turin to Genoa.*

Savona (anciently called *Sabatia* or *Sabatium*) is the second Town, or eldest Daughter of *Genoa*, and like a good Daughter indeed she stands always in her Mothers presence, yet keeps her distance; it being within sight of *Genoa*, yet five and twenty miles off. It stands upon the *Mediterranean Sea*, or, as they call it here, upon the *Riviera di Genoa*. It's fortified both by *Art* and *Nature*, that is, by regular Fortifications towards the Sea, and by lusty *Appennine* Hills towards the Land. Yet whilst *Savona* fear'd no danger from either Sea or Land, it was almost ruin'd in the year 1648, by Fire from Heaven, to wit, *Lightning*, which falling upon a great *Savona.*

Tower

Tower in the midst of the Town, where Gunpowder was kept, blew it up upon a sudden, and with it threw down two hundred Houses round about it, and Houses of note. For, passing that way six months after, and walking among the Ruins, I saw in many of the Houses, which were but half fallen down, curious painted Chambers, and fine gilt Roofs, which shew'd me of what House many of these Houses had been; and of what weak defence gilt Roofs and painted Walls are against the Artillery of Heaven, Thunder and Lightning.

This Town is famous in History for the Interview of two great Kings here, to wit, *Lewis* the XII. of *France*, and *Ferdinand* King of *Naples*. This Interview passed with demonstrations of mutual civilities, not ordinary in Interviews of Princes; for *Lewis* feared not to go into the Galleys and Ships of *Ferdinand* without Guards, and unarm'd; and *Ferdinand* remain'd for many days together in this Town, belonging then to *Lewis*, whom he had lately stripp'd of the Kingdom of *Naples*, and beaten him to boot in a Battel.

Of this Town were *Julius Secundus* and *Sixtus Quartus*, two Popes of the House of *Roueri*; and two great Cardinals, *Peter* and *Raphael Riarii*.

La Riviera di Genoa. Embarking at *Savona* in a Felucca, we row'd along the Shore (call'd *la Riviere di Genoa*) unto *Genoa* it self; and all the way long we saw such a continual Suburbs of stately *Villa's* and *Villages*, that these scantlings made us in love with the whole piece it self, *Genoa*. I confess, I never saw a more stately abord to any City than

than to this, and if we had not had *Genoa* full
in our sight all the way long, we should have taken some of these stately Villages for *Genoa* it
self, and have imitated *Hostingus*, the Leader of
the *Normans*, who coming into *Italy* about the
year 860, with a great Army, and finding *Luna*
(a Town in the Confines of *Genoa*) so sumptu-
ously built, thought really it had been *Rome*, and
thereupon taking it, he gloried that he had
sacked the Mistriss of the World ; *Gratatur te-* *Dreilo e*
nere se Monarchiam totius Imperii, per quem quam *S. Quintino*
putabat Romam, saith his Historian. *lib. 1, de*
Sailing thus along this pleasant Coast, we *morib. &*
came betimes to *Genoa*. *Ad. Norm.*

Genoa is one of the chief Towns that stands *Genoa.*
upon the *Mediterranean Sea*, and one of the best
in *Italy*; the common *Italian* Proverb calls it
Genua la Superba: and if ever I saw a Town
with its Holiday Clothes always on, it was
Genoa. It stands upon the side of a Hill, and
rising by degrees, appears to those that look
upon it from the Sea, like an Amphitheatre.
Heretofore it was only fortified by Marble
Bulwarks, that is, great Hills of Marble,
which backt it up, but some forty years ago it *The Walls.*
was environ'd with new Walls, carrying six
miles in compass, and yet finish'd in eighteen
months.

The Haven heretofore was very unsafe, and
many Ships which had tug'd through the most *The Haven*
dangerous Seas abroad, were seen to sink here
in the Haven and at home; the *French*, then Masters of *Genoa*, not suffering her to shut up her
Haven, lest she should shut them out. But since
she hath shaken off the French Yoke, she hath
lock-

locked up her Treaſures, and bolted the door on the inſide, by that admirable *Mola*, which croſſing almoſt quite over the Bay or Haven, doth not only bolt out all Enemies, but even locks up the boiſterous Sea it ſelf, and makes it tame in the Haven. It's a prodigious Work, and able to have puzzl'd any two Kings in *Europe* to have done it.

The Phares. At one end of this *Mola* ſtands the *Pharos*, upon a little rock, with a *Lantern* upon it, to give notice, by known ſigns, what Ships, how many, and from what ſide they come; or elſe to guide their own Ships home ſafely in the night. At firſt it was only a little Fort, that might help to bridle *Genoa*, and it was built by *Lewis* XIII. of *France*.

The City it ſelf. As for the Town it ſelf of *Genoa*, it's moſt beautiful to behold, many of the Houſes being painted on the outſide, and looking as if they were turned inſide out, and had their *Arras* Hangings hung on their outſides. The tops of their Houſes are made with open Galleries, where the Women ſit together at work in cluſters, and where alſo they dry their *Hair* in the Sun, after they have waſh'd it in a certain waſh us'd on purpoſe to make it yellow, a colour much affected here by all Women.

The Streets. The *Streets* are very narrow; ſo that they uſe here few Coaches, but many Sedans and Litters: this makes the noiſe in the Streets leſs and the expence in the Purſe ſmaller. But, for want of Ground and Earth, they make Heaven pay for it, taking it out in the heighth of their Houſes, what they want in breadth or length; ſo that *Genoa* look'd in my Eye like a proud a proud young Lady in a ſtrait-bodied flower'd Gown, which makes her look tall indeed and fine, but hinders her from being at her eaſe, and taking breath freely.

Yet I muſt except the *Strada Nova* here, which for a ſpirt ſurpaſſeth all the Streets I ever ſaw any where elſe for neatneſs and proportion ; and, if it had but Breath enough to hold out at the ſame rate a little longer, it would be the true *Queen-ſtreet* of *Europe* : Ordinary Houſes are ſo out of countenance here, that they dare not appear in this Street, where there's nothing but Palaces, and Palaces as fine as Art and Coſt, or as Marble and Painting, can make them.

Strada Nova.

Having ſaid thus much of *Genoa* in general, I will now come to the particulars that are to be ſeen in it.

1. The *Domo*, or great *Church* of St. *Lawrence*, preſents it ſelf to my ſight ; it's the Cathedral of the *Archbiſhop*. This Church is of a noble ſtructure, all of black and white Marble intermingled, and all maſſive ſquare Stones. In a Chapel over againſt the Pulpit is kept reverently an authentick Relick of St. *John Baptiſt*, under the Altar, as we are told ; and the great Diſh of one *Emerald*, in which, they ſay here, our Saviour eat the *Paſchal Lamb* with his Diſciples. Both theſe were given to the *Genoeſi* by *Baldwin* King of *Hieruſalem*, for their great Service done againſt the *Turks* in the *Holy Land*. Of the Relick of St. *John Baptiſt*, *Baronius* ſpeaks boldly in his Eccleſiaſtical Hiſtory ; But for the Diſh of *Emerald*, I find no Authority at all for it, either in *Baronius* or any other Author, that

The Domo.

Baron. ad An. 1101. n. 43.

our

our Saviour ufed it ; efpecially feeing venera-
Beda, l. de ble *Beda* writes, that the Difh in which our Sa-
ior. fanct. viour eat the *Paschal Lamb* was of Silver.
c. 2.

2. After the *Domo*, I faw the Church of the
The An- *Annunciata*, which draweth up the Ladder
nunciata. after it for neatnefs. It's ftill in building, and
not quite finifh'd. It's thus beautified at the
Gli Signori coft of two Brothers, rich Gentlemen, and
Lomelini. Merchants of this Town, who allow the third
part of their Gains to the adorning of this
Church. The Roof of it is all gilt, and fet
with curious Pictures in *Platfound* ; the Altars
round about the Church are checked with ex-
quifite Pillars, and adorn'd with rare pictures;
the two rows of *vaft Pillars* which hold up the
Roof of the Church, are fo beautiful, being of
a red and white Marble, that they look like
Jafper, and ravifh the beholders, whilft they
gaze on their curious Work.

S. Ambro- 3. The Church of S. *Ambrofio*, belonging to
fio. the *Jefuits*, is neatly overcrufted with Marble,
and gilt above in the Roof. It wants a little
length, for want of room to build on.; it being too near the *Doge*'s Palace, and not daring
to advance a ftep further, for fear of treading
upon his Heels.

S. Cyro. 4. The Church of the *Theatins*, call'd S. *Cyro*,
Is very handfom, with its double row of white
Marble Pillars, which fet it out very graceful-
ly. The Cloyfter alfo is very neat, and the
Fathers very civil.

Th: Pala- 5 The *Palaces* here are moft fumptuous :
ces. thofe of *Strada Nova* are the beft, and the beft
of thofe is that of the Prince *d' Oria* ; it's built
upon white round Marble Pillars, which fup-
port

port its Galleries, and thofe Galleries let you into noble Rooms, adorn'd with all the *Abeliimenti* of *Italian* Palaces. The other Palaces too in this Street deferve particular mention in this defcription of *Genoa*, and may take it Ill I fay nothing of them; but they muft excufe my brevity, and impute the fault partly to themfelves, feeing admirable things are liable to this inconvenience, that they are alfo unexpreffible.

6. I faw alfo the two Palaces of the *Signori Balbi*, in the Street of the *Annunciata*; In the one whereof (on the left hand) I faw, among other rich things, a Looking-glafs, valued at threefcore thoufand Crowns; it's much of the fize of thofe Looking-glaffes which *Seneca* calls *fpecula tori corpori paria*, that is, as big and brittle as thofe that look themfelves in them: the Frame of it is all of Silver, fet thick with a thoufand little armed Figures like *Cupids*, as if the plain Mirrour of this Looking-glafs were the plain Field where *Cupid* pitcheth his *Tents*, and begins his Conquefts over fair Ladies. The round Pillars fet in the Porch of this Houfe, and the *Giuochi di Acqua* in the Garden, will make themfelves be taken notice of.

The Palaces of Signori Balba.

7. The Palace of the *Doge*, or biennial Prince here, with the feveral *Chambers* of *Juftice*, and the *Armory* in it for thirty thoufand Men, ought to be carefully feen. In one of the great Halls of this *Palace* you have twelve *Statues* of white Marble, reprefenting twelve famous Men of this Town, who had render'd great Service to the Commonwealth. In the 'forefaid *Armory* you fee a Halbard with two Piftol-barrels in the

The Doges Palace.

The Armory.

the lower end of it. You fee alfo the Armour of the *Genoefian Amazons*, who went to the War in the *Holy Land*, and carried themfelves gallantly. Here's alfo a Cannon of Leather fo light, that a Man may carry it.

San Pietro in Arena. 8. But that which is the moſt taking in *Genoa*, is that which is out of *Genoa*, I mean, the ſtately Suburbs of *San Pietro* in *Arena*, where for a mile together Villa's adorn'd with Marbles, Painting, Statues, Gardens, Arbours of Gelſomin, Orange and Limon Trees, Grotts, Ponds, *Giuochi d'Acqua*, Fountains, high Walls, with Shades born up by Marble Pillars, *&c.* compos'd of many Palaces and Gardens, ſuch a beautiful Landskip, that the whole place ſeem'd to me to be the charming Paradiſe of the King of the *Mountains* anciently, and I was almoſt going to ſay, that we durſt not bleſs our ſelves, leſt this enchanted place ſhould have vaniſh'd. The beſt Villa's or Palaces here, are thoſe of *Hieronymo Negro*; and that of the *Imperiali*; the firſt beautified with all the graces of *Italian* Furniture, as alſo with Gardens, Walks, Ponds, Water-works, Allys, *&c.* the other, beſides all theſe, hath an excellent proſpect; for the Maſter of this Houſe can ſee out of one Window of it, Twelve thouſand Crowns a year of his own, only in let Houſes. The other Palaces here expect I ſhould ſay ſomething of them, and they deſerve it well; but really, to give them their full due, I can only ſay this of them, That they ought to be ſeen by the Eye, not deſcribed by the Pen.

9. As

9. As you return from *San Pietro in Arena* to the Town, not far from the Gates, stands the Villa, or Palace of the Duke *d' Oria*. I reserved this for the last, *pour faire bonne bouche*. It stands upon the Seaside, and its Garden towards the Sea is built upon three rows of *white Marble Rails*, born up by *white marble Pillars*, which ascending by degrees, is so beautiful to behold from the Sea, that Strangers passing that way to *Genoa*, take this Garden for a second *Paradise*. In the midst of it stands the rare *Fountain of Neptune*, representing the true looks of brave *Andrea d' Oria*, the *Neptune* of the *Ligurian Sea*, and the man who put his Country out of Livery, and taught it not to serve. All along one side of this Garden stands a *Cage* of *Iron*, about a hundred paces long, and so high, that it fetcheth in a world of Laurel and other Trees, clad with chirping Birds of several sorts; and, to make the poor Birds believe that they are rather in a Wood than in a Prison, the very Cage hath put even the Wood itself in Prison. Then entring into the Palace, we found it most curiously adorn'd with Rarities and Riches suitable to the Country's humor and the Master's purse. It's true, when this Queen of *Spain* passed from *Germany* into *Spain*, by way of *Milan* and *Genoa*, the *Governor* of *Milan* told her, that she should see in *d'Oria's* Palace here many fine things, but all borrow'd of the Townsmen. Which *d'Oria* hearing of beforehand, caused to be written over the great Gates of the Palace, where the Queen was to enter and lodge, these words in Spanish, *By the Grace of God, and the King's Favour, there's nothing here borrow'd*. It may be the

The Villa of the Duke d'Oria.

F   cun-

Part I. A Voyage to ITALY.

of Blood, which ran in the very Streets of *Genoa*. It had like to have swam a second time in its Blood, when *Lewis* XII. of *France* entering into *Genoa* victoriously with Sword in hand threatning the utter ruine of that People, was pacified by the mournful Cries of Four thousand little Children, who, clad in Sackcloth, and placed in the great *Piazza*, cry'd out to the King in a piercing accent, *Misericordia è Pietà, Mercy and Pity*. But since *Genoa* shook off the French Yoke, it hath lived perpetually jealous of the French, especially since it discover'd, some years past, divers attempts of *France* against it, whilst the French had *Portolongone* and *Piombino*.

For this reason the *Genoefi* lean much to the Spanish Faction; and Fashions following Factions they lean much to the Spanish Fashion both in Humor and Apparel. Hence I found here broad Hats without Hatbands, broad Leather Girdles with Steel Buckles, narrow Breeches, with long-waisted Doublets and hanging-sleeves to be *a la mode*, as well as in *Madrid*. And I found all the great Ladies here to go like the Donna's of *Spain*, in * *Guardinfanta's*; that is, in horrible overgrown Fartingals of Whalebone, which being put about the Waist of the Lady, and full as broad on both sides as she can reach with her hands, bear out her Coats in such a huffing manner, that she appears to be as broad as long. I was told by one of their Noblemen, that a certain Lady of a Noble House, when her Son was a condemn'd Prisoner, deliver'd him both from Captivity and Death, by taking him under her *Guardinfanta's*,

* *Child-preserver.*

F 2

fanta's, and carrying him thence, supported by her Women, from whence she could privately send him out of the State. So that the Men here with their little close Breeches looked like Tumblers that leap through the Hoops; and the Women like those that danced anciently the *Hobby-horse* in Country Mummings.

Their Riches.

As for their *Riches*, I am told they pass not a Million and two hundred thousand Crowns a year. Indeed the *King* of *Spain*, *Philip* the II. above a hundred years ago, borrowed of this *Republick* the sum of eleven Millions, and keeps them still in his hands to keep this *Republick* in awe; yet paying the interest duly unto them. So that the *Common Purse* here, is nothing so rich as that of *Venice*, though the particular Men here are far richer than those of *Venice*. They have great Trading both with *France* and *Spain*; and are great *Bankiers*, making the *Change* in all the Banks of *Europe*, go as they please. Besides they utter a world of *Taffataes, Velvets, Sataius, Points* of needle work, and divers other things of Value.

Their Strength.

As for their *Strength*, it's enough to defend themselves, scarce enough to offend others. For *Genoua* is back'd up by the *Appennines*, where all passages are easily made good against Invaders; and it is so well fortified on the other side by the *Sea* it self, twelve or fourteen good Gallies, twenty Ships of War, and it's incomparable *Molo*, that they could scuffle notably in their own defence. Besides, *Genoua* is fortified not only with its Hills and Sea, but also with its new *Walls* and bull-warks of *Stone*; nay, and with its *Bone-walls* too, that is, with

a La-a *Lacedemonian Wall* of a world of Inhabitants, and with the illustrious Families of *d' Oria*, *Spinola*, *Grimaldi*, *Sauli*, *Duraxxi*, *Catanei*, and others, whose several names would go almost for several Armies. Yet for a need, they can raise thirty thousand Men, and arm them well out of their *Arsenal*. I confess heretofore they were strong enough to offend others; for they made War against the *Pisani*, and worsted them: They set also upon the *Island* of *Corsica*, distant from *Genoa* about a hundred miles, and took it. This Island gave the *Republick* of *Genoa* more honour than profit: for, it being once a Kingdom, gives still to *Genoa* the Title of *Serenissima*, and a *Close Regal Crown* over its *Coat of Arms*. In fine, the *Genoeses* were strong enough heretofore, to lend great Succours to *Godfry* of *Bulen* in his holy Conquest of *Hierusalem*. Hence upon the very *Area* of the *Holy Sepulchre* in *Hierusalem*, are written these words: *Præpotens Genoensium præsidium*.

As for their Interest, it seemed to me to be far more *Spanish* than *French*, by reason of the great profit they draw from *Spain*, which corresponds with the rich State of *Milan* in Men and Moneys, by means of the *Genoese*: yet they are well with all Christian Princes, except with the Duke of *Savoy*, who pretends to *Savona*.

As for the learned men of this Town, I find them not to be so many. The rich *Banquier* is more-esteemed here, than the learned *Divine*. Yet I find here also some famous for learning, to wit, *Baptista Fregosus*, or *Fulgosus*, who for his singular parts being chosen *Doge* of *Genoa*, and by his own disloyal kindred chafed from Government and Country, comforted himself in his Studies; and having observed many particular things in History, he reduced them to Heads, and left us a just volume of Memorable Sayings and Deeds of the Antients: for which work, he is stiled by *Alberto Leandro*, the *Valerius Maximus* of *Italy*. He wrote in *Italian*, and dedicated his Book to his Son. The other learned Men of this Town are *Justinianus*, *Balus*, *Mascardi*, and *Christopher Columbus*.

Genoa also hath given to the Church of *Rome* three *Popes*, *Adrian* the V. *Innocent* the IV. and *Innocent* the VIII.

The Academy of Wits. Here is an *Academy of Wits* called the *Adormentati*; which together with the other *Academies* of the like nature in all the Towns of *Italy*, I would wish my *Traveller* to visit particularly, that he may see how far the *Italians* excel us, in passing their time well; and how it's much better to spend the week in making of *Orations* and *Verses*, than in drinking of *Ale* and smoaking of Tobacco.

Their Historian. He that desires to know more of *Genoa*, let him read *Augustinus Justinianus* of the History of *Genoa*.

Having spent six days in *Genoa*, we agreed with an honest *Vetturino* to conduct us to *Asilan*, which is about four little days journey from hence. In another Voyage I went from *Genoa* *Monferrat.* to *Turin* by *Montferrat*, and saw in my way *Novi* (of which by and by) *Trino Cassale*, one *Cassal.* of the strongest places of *Italy*, having a strong *Cittadell*, a strong *Castle*, strong Town-walls and

and Ditches; and *Alexandria della Paglia*, a *Alexandria*
ſtrong Town ſtanding upon the *Po*.

But now at this time leaving *Genoa*, and intending for *Milan*, we rid through *San Pietro d' Arena*, by the *Carthuſians Monaſtery*, over the *Apennine Hills*, and in a day and a half came to *Novi*.

Novi is a little ſtrong Town belonging to the *Novi*. *Genoeſi*, and Frontier to *Milaneſi*. It's ſome twelve Miles diſtant from *Tortona*, the firſt Frontier Town of the State of *Milan* : and becauſe theſe Frontiers were then peſter'd with *Bandits*, a Nobleman of *Genoa*, who was in our company, begg'd of the *Governour* of *Novi* a Convoy for himſelf and us, to ſecure us to *Tortano* : The Governour preſently granted us a Convoy of eight or ten Horſe-men : but, thoſe very Men he gave us for our Convoy, were *Bandits* themſelves, who being baniſhed from the State and Town of *Genoa* for their miſdemeanors, had two Months a year allowed them to come freely into Frontier Towns, and negotiate with the State. Theſe Men were thought by the Governor to be our ſafeſt Guards in danger. Having been thus convoyed by our honeſt Rogues paſt all danger, we paid them ſome three Piſtoles; and feared no more danger, till we ſhould meet with ſuch Servants as theſe another time. I confeſs, it ſeemed at firſt a fearful thing, to ſee our ſelves in the hands of thoſe, who had their hands often in Blood: yet there is ſuch a charm in a Governors Parole; that we thought our ſelves as well armed with it, as if we had been ſhot-free, and had had all the *Spells* of *Lapland* about us.

Tortona. We had no sooner parted from these our Guards, but passing over a little River on Horseback, we entred into the *Milanese*, and came at night to *Tortona*, a strong Frontier Town of the *Milanese*, where *Charles* the VIII. of *France*, in his return from the Conquest of *Naples*, beat the *Venetians*, and the *Milanesi* in a Battle.

Pavia. From *Tortona* we went the next day to *Pavia*, the second Town of the State of *Milan*, and once the Seat of twelve Kings of the *Lon-*
Ticinum. *gobards*. It stands upon the River *Ticinum*, and hence it's also called in Latin *Ticinum*. Here's an University, either founded or furnished at first, with Readers, or by Readers of the University of *Oxford*. The chief Colleges,
The Domo. are, that of *Pius Quintus*, and that of *S. Charles Borromæus*. The other remarkable things here, are, 1. The *Domo*, in which lieth buried the Body of a holy Bishop of this Town, called *Sauli*, who was contemporary to *S. Charles Borromæus*, and of the same spirit and zeal. Near the great door of this Church (on the inside) they shew you a little *Mast* of a *Boat*, which they make ignorant people believe (for sport) to have been the Lance of *Orlando Furioso*.

The Equestris Statua of Antoninus. 2. Near the *Domo*, in the *Piazza*, stands a *Brazen Statue*, which some affirm to be the Statue of *Constantine* the Great; others, more probably, of *Antoninus Pius*. It was brought from *Ravenna* hither by Victory; and it had like to have been carried back again to *Ravenna* by Victory. For *Lotrech* the *French General* in the taking of this Town, having granted this
Statue

Statue to a Soldier of *Ravenna* (who served under him, and who having mounted the Breach first, asked nothing for his recompence but that *Statue*, taken antiently from his Native Town.) Yet afterwards moved with the generosity of the Townsmen (who having left all things else with some patience, to the prey of the Souldiers, burst into Tears, when they heard that this *Statue* was to be taken from them.) *Lotrech* changed his Gift to the Souldier, and left the Citizens of *Pavia* their dear *Statue*.

3. I saw the *Augustins Church*, where the Body of that great Father of the Church S. *Augustin* lieth buried. It was translated hither out of *Sardinia* by *Luitprandus King* of the *Longobardi*; an Arm of which S. *Augustin* a *King* of *England* redeemed at a great rate, and yet cheap too, if it were his writing Arm, wherewith he wrote such admirable Books. The new *Tomb* in the *Sacristy* is all of white Marble, most exquisitely carved with Historical Statues representing the most remarkable actions of that Doctor.

S. *Augustins Body.*
Baron. an. 725.
Baron. an. 1025.

4. In the same Church we were shown the *Tomb* of *Severinus Boetius*, Author of that great little Book *de Consolatione Philosophica*, which he wrote in his Exile, to comfort himself. He was a *Consul* of *Rome* for dignity, another St. *Denys* for Learning and Losing his Head: and held a Martyr by many.

The Tomb of Severinus Boetius. See Baron. an. 525.

5. In the Cloister of this Convent of the *Augustins*, lie buried two *Englishmen* of note, the *Duke* of *Suffolk*, and an *English Bishop* called *Parker*, of the House of *Morley*, upon whose Tombs are handsome Epitaphs.

6. The

6. The Chapel where the *Bones* of the *Frenchmen* killed in the *Battle* of *Pavia* are kept and shown to Strangers.

7. In the *Franciscans Church* here, lies buried *Baldus* the famous Jurisconsult.

8. The long *Wooden-Bridge*, covered over head with a perpetual Penthouse, to defend men as well from the Sun, as from the Rain.

Learned Men. Of this Town were *Ennodius* *Ticinensis*, and *Lanfrancus*, Archbishop of *Canterbury*, who wrote against *Berengarius* for the *Real Presence*.

The History. He that desires to know the particular History of *Pavia*, let him read *Antonio Spelta*, and *Sacco*.

From *Pavia* we went to *Milan*, some twenty miles off; and in the way, saw the famous *Monastery* of the *Carthusians*, near unto which, upon S. *Matthias* his day (a day favourable to *Charles* the V. seeing he was *born* on that day, *Crowned Emperor* on that day, and got *this Victory* on that day) was fought that memorable Battle between the said Emperours Forces, and the *French King*, Anno 1525. where *The Battle of Pavia.* *Francis* the I. of *France* was taken Prisoner, having lost the day, not for want of courage, but conduct: for he had a little before, sent away half of his Army to the Conquest of *Naples*; by which he so weakened the rest of his Army here, that he both lost the day, and did nothing against the Kingdom of *Naples*; a great fault observed by one that was present there, to wit, *See Monluc's Commentaries.* *Monsieur Monluc*. *Francis* being thus taken prisoner, was presently conducted to the *Carthusian Monastery*, which was hard by. Entering into the *Church*, and finding the *Monks* sing-

singing in the *third hour* this verſe of the *Pſalm*, *Coagulatum eſt ſicut lac cor eorum, ego vero legem ſuam meditatus ſum*, he ſtruck up with them at the next *verſe*, and ſung aloud with a piety as great as his loſs, or courage, *Bonum mihi quia humiliaſti me, ut diſcam juſtificationes tuas*: that is, it's well for me, that thou haſt humbled me, that I may learn thy *Juſtifications*. After he had heard *Maſs* here, he was carried to Dinner in the *Monaſtery*, and was ſerved by three Generals of the *Spaniſh Army*, *Launoy*, *Bourbon*, and the *Marquis* of *Vaſti*; the one holding the Baſin, the ſecond pouring *Water* upon his hands, and the third preſenting him the *Towel*. Some ſay he refuſed to be ſerved by *Bourbon*, looking upon him as a revolted Traytor, rather than as an Enemy: indeed the brave *French Knight Bayard* (ſirnamed the *Chevalier ſans peur*, who died in the Battle,) being found expiring in the Field by *Bourbon*, who ſaid to him, *Poor Bayard! I pity thee*; anſwered him with all the courage and life that was left him; *No, Traytor, I am not to be pitied, who die nobly, ſerving my King and Country: but, thou rather art to be pitied, who liveſt a Traytor to thy King and Country*. As for the King he was led Priſoner into *Spain*, where he was kept at *Madrid* till he paid his Ranſom. Hence the *Spaniards* brag, that they had once a *French King* Priſoner, and the *French* had never any King of *Spain* Priſoner: but the *French* anſwer; that their King had not been Priſoner had he fought as the Kings of *Spain* do of late, that is, by *Proxy*, and not in Perſon. However this *Francis* the firſt deſerved better Fortune, being a Prince of great

Cou-

Courage and Honour, and a great lover of his Soldiers. For not long before, he had beaten the *Swiſſers* in the Battle of *San Doniro*, where his Soldiers fought for him with singular Courage and Zeal. And he had deserved it all: For he was so good to his Soldiers in that expedition, that he would ride up and down the Camp in the night to visit the wounded Soldiers, and help them to all necessaries, commanding even His own *ſheets* to be cut in pieces to bind up their Wounds.

The Car-thuſians Monaſtery. As for the Monaſtery it ſelf of the *Carrbuſians*, it's one of the moſt ſtately Monaſteries of *Italy*, and, I believe, the ſecond of that *Order*. The great Cloiſter is all covered with Lead. The Church is one of the handſomeſt of *Italy* though built *a la Tedeſca*. The Frontiſpiece of it is adorned with a world of *Heads* and *Figures* of white marble. The *Chapels* within are richly adorned and painted. The *Tabernacle* is worth fourſcore thouſand Crowns. The Tomb of their *Founder*, *John Galeazzo Viſcounti*, *Duke* of *Milan*, which ſtands a little without the *Quire*, with the *cumbent Statues* of *Ludovico Moro* the laſt *Duke* of *Milan* and his *Wife*, lying under the other, is a ſtately *Monument*. In the *Sacriſty* we were ſhown many fine *Relicks*, much rich *Church-plate*, and the curious back of an *Altar* of *Ivory* cut into Hiſtories after a rare manner.

Milan. Paſſing from hence we came to *Milan*. This Town is ſurnamed the *Great*; and rightly, ſeeing it carries full ten miles in compaſs within the Walls. It hath ten Gates to it; two hundred Churches within it, and three hundred thou-

Part I. *A Voyage to* ITALY. 77

thousand souls dwelling in it. Hence it was an- *The Dutchy*
tiently called *Altera Roma* a second *Rome*, both *of Milan.*
because of its Greatness, and because of its
other Titles, which made it look like *Rome*.
It's the Head of the best *Dutchy* in *Europe*,
which is a hundred miles long from *North* to
South, and containeth four hundred *Towns* in it.
It's called *Miland quasi Midland*, being a pure
Mediterranean Town, and having (which is a
wonder not so much as a River of its own running in it; but is only served by two Channels
cut out of the *Ticine* and the *Adder*. This Town
hath heretofore suffered much by War; great
Towns being the fairest marks to shoot at,
and *Milan* hath been forty times shot at by
Sieges, and twenty times hit, and taken, having had the misfortune to have been under
divers Factions and Rulers: as the Emperours,
the *Turriani*, the *Visconti*, the *Sforze*, the
French and the *Spaniards*, who now keep it,
mersé al Castello, which staveth off all attempts of Strangers. *France* pretends to this
Dutchy as Heir of *Valentia Visconty*, who was
married to *Lewis* Duke of *Orleans*, whose house
was excluded from this Dutchy by *Francis Sforza*, who possessed himself of this State.

As for the things which I saw in *Milan*, they
are these.

1. A great number of Genty and Nobility *Store of*
here, which I perceived to be very numerous, *Gentry.*
because of an hundred Coaches (no Hackneys)
which I saw standing before a Church upon a
private *Festival-day* of that Church.

2. Great

2. Great store of *Artizans*, as Goldsmiths, Armourers, Gunsmiths, Weavers, Silkstocking-makers, Refiners of Gold, those that work in Crystal, and a world of others; which gives occasion to the Proverb, which saith, That *he that would improve all* Italy, *must destroy* Milan *first*; for if *Milan* were destroy'd, the many Artizans that are there, would spread over all *Italy*, and furnish the other Towns, which want Artizans.

Store of Artizans.

3. The *Churches* here, and first that of S. *Ambrose*, where that glorious Father of the *Church* refus'd stoutly to *Theodosius* the *Emperor*, entrance into that *Church*, because of his passionate commanding the Massacre at *Thessalonica*, where seven thousand Men were murder'd for the fault of a few. Under the high Altar of this Church lieth the Body of S. *Ambrose*, as also the Bodies of *Gervasius* and *Protasius*, two primitive Saints, whose Bodies were said to be found whilst S. *Austin* liv'd at *Milan*, and who also relates a famous Miracle, which, they say, was known to have been wrought by God, at the translation of those holy Martyrs Bodies into this *Church*. In this *Church* also is seen upon a high Pillar of a round form, a Brazen Serpent, like that erected by *Moses* in the *Desart*, and commanded by God himself to be made: I imagine it was set up here for the same end for which it was commanded by God to be set up mystically in the Desart, that is, to put Men in mind of our Saviour's exaltation upon the Cross for Mankind, the frequent memory of which is a soveraign Antidote against the stings of the infernal Serpent, the Devil.

S. Ambrose's Church.

S. Ambrose his Tomb.

Read S. Augustin, lib. 9. Conf. c. 7.

Numb. 21. 8.

John 3. 1, 4.

4. Near

Part I.   A Voyage to ITALY.   79

4. Near unto the 'foresaid Church of S. *Ambrose* stands the little *Chapel*, where S. *Augustin* with his little *Adeodatus*, and his Friend *Alippius*, was baptiz'd, as the Words over the Altar testifie; and from this little *Chapel* it's said S. *Ambrose* and S. *Augustin* (then become *Christians*) going processionally to the *great Church*, made the Hymn *Te Deum*, as they went, one making one Verse, the other another. *The Hymn Te Deum.*

5. The other little *Chapel* on the other side of S. *Ambrose's Church*, is built upon the place where S. *Augustin* was first converted by a Voice, which said to him, *Tolle lege, Tolle lege :* meaning S. *Paul's* Epistles: Which he doing, pitch'd just upon those Words to the *Romans*, *Non in cubilibus & impudicitiis, sed induimini Jesum Christum*, &c. And so of an impure *Manichean* he became a chaste *Christian*. *The place of the Conversion of S. Austin.*

6. I saw adjoyning to this *Church* of S. *Ambrose*, the stately Monastery, with *two* curious Cloysters built upon round Pillars. The Monastery, as well as S. *Ambrose's* Church, belongs to the *Cistertian Monks*. *The Cistertians Monastery.*

7. Then I saw the Church of S. *Victor*, belonging to the *Olivetan Fathers*, with the admirable Picture of S. *George* killing the *Dragon*, of the hand of *Raphael Urbin*. This is a neat *Church* when it is adorn'd in its best Hangings, as it was when I *saw* it. The double Cloysters here of the Monastery, built upon round Pillars, ought to be seen. *S. Victor his Church.*

8. In the Church of S. *Nazarius* are to be seen the Tombs of the *Trivultii*; stately Monuments. *S. Nazario*

9. In

80   A Voyage to ITALY.   Part I.

S. Eustor-gio.   9. In the Church of S. *Eustorgius* I saw the *Arca*, or old Tomb, in which reposed the Bodies of the three *Magi* who came to adore our Saviour in *Bethlem*, whose Bodies were said to be tranflated from hence to *Colen* in *Germany*, where I have seen them, by reason of the destruction of *Milan*.

10. I saw also the Church of S. *Lawrence*, built like that of *Sancta Sophia* in *Constantinople*. Here lies buried *Placidia*, the Sister of *Honorius* the Emperor.

11. There are divers other Churches here, all worth particular visiting, by reason of some rare thing in them; as in that of S. *Mark*, the rare piece of *Simon Magus*'s fall from the Skies. In that of the Passion, the rare Picture of the last Supper, by *Christophoro Cibò*. In that of S. *Celso*, a rare Picture of *Raphael*'s hand in the Sacristy. The *Theatins* and the *Jesuits* Churches are very neat.

The Domo.   12. But the best of all the Churches of *Milan* is the new *Domo*, in the midst of which lieth buried the new S. *Ambrose* of *Milan*; I mean S. *Charles Borromæus*, another S. *Ambrose* in Pastoral Dignity, Zeal and Sanctity. This Church I take to be the second in *Italy* for solid work, being built all of white Marble, with Isles and Pillars, each Pillar worth ten thousand crowns, and there are a hundred and threescore such Pillars in all, of massive white Marble, not candied and frozen over with a thin crust of Marble, as most of the other fine Churches of *Italy* are. There are also six hundred white Marble Statues set round about the outside of this Church, each of them cost a thousand crowns.

S. Lorenzo.

That

Part I.   *A Voyage to* ITALY.   81

That of S. *Bartholomeus*, with his Skin upon his Arm, and that of *Adam*, are two pieces much admir'd, and are of the hand of *Christophoro Cibo*. The Frontispiece is not yet finish'd, but if that be the true design of it, which I have seen in Pictures in the *Capuchins* Cloyster in *Rome*, it will be most stately. The Church it self is said to be 250 cubits long. Near the Quire, and almost in the middle of the Church, lieth the Body of S. *Charles Borromæus*, in a low Vault, turn'd now into a Chapel, open at the top, with low Rails round about it: The inside of this Chapel is hung with Hangings of Cloth of Gold, over which runs a Cornish of *silver Plate* nailed to the Wall. Upon the Altar lieth the Body of S. *Charles* at length in a fair *Crystal Coffin* made of several great Squares of Crystal, thro' which (the wooden Case being open'd by special leave from the Archbishop) we saw his Body lying all along in his *Episcopal Robes*; his Face, Hands, and Feet are only seen, and his *Nose* and *Lips* are shrunk and parched. The true Picture of this Saint hangs at the entrance below into this Chapel, and his History and wonderful Actions are hung up in painting round about the Church, on high. Over the high Altar, in the very Roof of the Church, is kept one of the *Nails* of the *Cross* of our *Saviour*, given anciently to the *Milanesi*, by the Emperor *Theodosius*. There burn always before it a number of little Lamps, set crosswise, and drawn up thither with a Pulley, to shew the people where that holy Relick is. In fine, the Steeple of this Church is not to be forgotten, it's not quite finish'd yet, but it's high

The Holy Nail.

G   enough

enough to tire any man, and to shew him from the top of it the whole Town of *Milan*, the whole compass and circumference of the rare Castle, and the whole Country round about for twenty miles on every side; a sight so pleasant, that I would wish my Traveller not only to mount up to the top of this Steeple, but (for this Steeples sake) to make it his constant practise (as I did) to mount up the chief Steeple of all great Towns.

The Hospital. 13. The great *Hospital*, built in a quadrangle upon arches and round pillars, is a most magnificent thing. Really, if Sickness were not a little unwholesome and troublesome; a Man would almost wish to be a little sick here, where a King, tho' in health, might lodge handsomly. The place where the sick people are kept, is built cross-wise, and in the middle of that cross stands an open Altar, where all the sick people from their several quarters, and from their very beds, may hear the Divine Service at once. Four thousand Men are entertained daily in this Hospital, and therefore it hath great Revenues. S. *Charles* was a great Benefactor to it; and gave away to it and other pious uses, in half an hour, five and twenty thousand crowns of Inheritance, which were fallen to him (being a man of eminent birth) half an hour before. Indeed he had no other Wife than his *Church*, nor other Children than the *Poor*.

The Seminary, The College of the Swissers. 14. The stately *Seminary*, and the College for the *Swissers*, are noble Buildings, and the eternal Works of S. *Charles*.

15. The

Part I. *A Voyage to* ITALY.

15. The *Lazaretto* is a vast Building, carrying in compass a thousand and eight hundred yards. It stands near the Town Walls, yet out of the Town, and is to receive into it those that are sick of the Plague. There are as many Chambers in it as there are Days in the Year. In the middle of the square of this vast Court, or Quadrangle, stands a round Chapel, cover'd at the top, but open on all sides in such a manner, as that all the People, from their several Chambers and Beds, may behold the Priest saying Divine Service, and joyn their Devotions to his. I have read in the life of S. *Charles Borromæus*, that in a Plague time he visited those that were infected, and ministred the holy Sacraments to them himself in person, and went in a solemn Procession in the head of the Clergy, with a Rope about his Neck, and barefoot, upon the Stones, to move stony Hearts to repentance, and to appease the Wrath of God, angry with his People.

The Lazzaretto.

16. The *Bibliotheca Ambrosiana* is one of the heft Libraries in *Italy*, because it is not so coy as the others, which scarce let themselves be seen; whereas this opens its Doors publickly to all comers and goers, and suffers them to read what Book they please. It was begun to be built by S. *Charles*, and continued by his Nephew Cardinal *Frederico Borromæo*; but it was much augmented since by the accession of *Vincentius Pinelli*'s Books, which, after his death, being ship'd by his Heirs for *Naples*, and taken by the *Turks*, were many of them thrown overboard by those *Analphabet Rogue*, who looked for other Merchandise than Books; yet many

The Library.

G 2 of

of them were recover'd again for Money, and set up here. Over the heads of the highest Shelves are set up the Pictures of learned men, a thing of more cost than profit, seeing with that cost many more Books might have been bought, and learned men are best seen in their Books and Writings: *Loquere ut te videam.*

The Gallery of Pictures. 17. Behind the Library stands the *Gallery* of Pictures, where I saw many choice *Originals* of prime Masters, and some exquisite Copies, as those four pieces of the *four Elements,* which certainly are copied after those that I describ'd above, in the House of the Duchess of *Savoy* near *Turin,* called *La Valentine.* But the rarest Piece of all, either in the *Library* or here, is the rare Manuscript kept here, of *Alberto Dureo.* Three hundred pounds have been refused for it.

The Dominicans Library. 18. The *Dominicans* Library is very considerable too: But you must not omit to see the Refectory here, where you shall find an admirable Picture of the Last Supper, made by rare *Laurentius Vincius:* The painted Cloyster here deserves a Visit too.

The Gratie. 19. The Monastery also called the *Gratie,* is one of the best in *Europe,* in whose Church is a rare picture of Christ crown'd with Thorns, of the hand of *Titian.*

The Cabinet of Canonico Serali. 20. The famous Gallery and Curiosities of *Canonico Serali,* far better than that of Monsieur *Servier* in *Lyons,* of which above. And here I wish my Pen were as ingenious to describe all the rare things of this *Gallery,* as the noble *Canon Serali* hath been in gathering them, and courteous in shewing them: some of these curious

Part I. A Voyage to ITALY,

rious things I yet remember, for my Reader's fake; as, a great variety of *Burning-glasses*, and yet not *Convex*, as ours ordinarily are, one of them set fire presently to a piece of board an inch thick that was brought forth. 2. A *Mandragora*. 3. A Bird without Feet, called by *Aristotle*, *Apodes*. 4. A Stone, out of which is drawn a thread, which being spun and woven, makes a Stuff-like Linnen, but of an incombustible nature: The Stone is called *Asbestos*, and the Stuff *Amyanthus*, which being foul and soil'd, is not to be made clean by washing in Water, but by throwing into the Fire. *Baltazar Bonifacius* in his *Historia Ludicra* tells of many who had such Stuff. 5. A world of rare Medals of the old Consuls and Emperors in Silver, Gold, and Brass. 6. A world of wooden things, as also Fruits and *Fungi*, all putrefied and turned into Stone, and yet no Metamorphosis neither, the things retaining their pristine forms. 7. Divers curious Clocks, whereof one shews the time of the day (strange) even in the *night* by a *quadrant*. 8. The little round *Cabinet*, flat above like a Child's Drum, with a smooth Glass; the Master setting little Ships, Coaches, &c. upon the Glass, they wheel and move up and down as it were of themselves, when all is done by a sympathetical vertue, and by the Master's turning secretly a little Wheel, where there is fasten'd some Loadstone, and the little Ships and Coaches having also some piece of Iron in their bottoms which touch the Glass, and so the Iron running after the Loadstone moved by the Wheel, makes these Ships and Coaches seem to move of themselves. 9. A piece of a *Thunderbolt*,

G 3　　　　which

which the Canon himself said he cut out of a Man's Thigh strucken with it. 10. Livers pieces of Coral just as it grows in the Sea. 11. A little Pillar two handful high, of Marble, so cracked, that it gapeth wide on one side with the crack, and is yet firmly united on the other. 12. A world of rich *Jewels*, strange *Stones*, *Camoes*, *Pictures*, *Crystals*, little *Infants in Wax* in glass Cases, and many other exotick Rarities, which are better seen than described.

Some Palaces. 21. There are some Palaces here; as that of the *Governers*, rather vast than curious, and fitter to lodge *Regiments of Guards* in, than *Viceroys*. The Palace of *Marini* is of a noble structure: That of the Archbishop is very handsom. I saw also the Palace of the *Borromei* painted within at the entrance, with the *Motto* of S. *Charles*, (who was of this Family) HUMILITAS. It's related in the Life of this holy Prelate, that in twenty years space that he was Archbishop and Cardinal here, he went but twice to visit his own near Relations in this Palace, and descended but twice into his own Garden in his Archiepiscopal Palace. The *Palaces* also of the *Visconti* of the *Sforza*, of the *Trivulzii*, and many others, deserve to be seen.

The Castle. 22. The *Castle* or *Cittadelle* is one of the best in *Europe*, in the opinion of the Duke of *Rohan*, who was a competent Judge. It is situate on the back of the Town, and commands on every side. It's guarded by a Garrison of five hundred natural *Spaniards*, with a special *Governor* of its own, independant of the Governor of *Milan*. It looks more like a Town than a Castle, being a mile and a half about, and furnish'd

Part I.   A Voyage to ITALY.   87

nish'd with all Conveniences a Soldier can require. The large Streets in it, the stately Houses and Palaces for the chief Commanders, the neat Piazza's, the number of well-furnish'd Shops in all kinds, even Goldsmiths too, the five Fountains or Wells not to be dried up, the Mill, the Hospital; the Church, with eight or ten Chaplains in it, and a Curate; the fair place of Arms, capable of six thousand Men; two hundred great pieces of Canon upon the Walls; the six Royal Bastions, the regular Fortifications or Outworks; the underground way from one Bastion to another; the infinite heaps of Cannon bullets, some whereof weigh 800 pound weight; the three large and deep Ditches round about the Castle; the stately Entrance, Gate, and two strong Towers, make this Castle one of the most Cavalier Curiosities a Man can see in *Italy*. They shew'd me here the Cannon which kill'd Mareschal *Crequy* before *Breme*, and for that Service it's allow'd to rest here for ever.

23. The Shops of Crystals, where you have *The Shops.* a world of Curiosities in Crystal; as Watch-cases, Twizer-cases, little Boxes, Pictures cut in Crystal, Crosses and Beads of Crystal, &c. The Shops also of Silk-stockings, which are hugely esteem'd in *Italy*, because they are twice as strong as ours, and very massive. The Shops, in fine, of *Embroiderers*, whose Embroidery in Gold and Silver is the best in the World, and the cheapest.

24. Here is an *Academy of Wits*, call'd the *The Academy* *Nascosti*, or *Hidden Men*. But why hidden? *of Wits.* *Wit*, like the Sun, should shine publickly, and

G 4   not

not bury it felf, except it be to fhew us, that as the Sun never fhines brighter than after he hath been hidden in a Cloud, fo Wit never fhines more, than after it hath been hidden in Study. Hence was that Saying of a grave Philofopher, *abfconde vitam,* that is, *lye hidden a while, at the Dug of the Book.* Indeed *Demofthenes* caufed his Hair to be fhaved off, that by that Deformity he might be afham'd to go abroad, and fo be obliged to ftudy at home. As for this Academy, it helps much to animate with Wit this great Town, which otherwife would look like *Polyphemus*, (having loft his Eye) great, but blind ; *Tumor non eft magnitudo.*

The learned Men. 25. The moft famous Men of this Town for learning have been thefe : *Valerius Maximus* for Hiftory ; *Alciatus, Decius* and *Jafon,* for Law ; *Cardan* for Philofophy ; *Panigarola* and *Paulus Arefius* for Sermons ; *Bonacina* for Canon Law ; and *Octavius Ferrarius* (whom I knew lately in *Padua*) for *belle lettere.*

A ftrong body. Leandro Alberto. 26. Two other Men here are famous for other things, to wit, *Uberto Crucio,* and *Gulielmo. Pufterula* ; the firft fo ftrong, that he could ftop a Horfe in his full gallop with one hand, lift up upon his Back a Horfe laden with Corn, and ftand fo ftifly upon his Legs that no Man, tho' running againft him with all his force, could pufh him out of his place or pofture.

A ftrong mind. The other without any Learning at all, except his firft Grammar Rudiments, could with his natural Wit only, decide Law-cafes, and make fuch good Orders, that the beft Lawyers could not find what to add to them. It's
pity

pity thefe two Men had not been melted into one, to have made one excellent Man, by their clubbing *Wit* and *Force* together, and their mingling of *Sana mens* with *Corpore fano*.

The *Revennes* that *Spain* draws from *Milan* yearly are two millions and four hundred thoufand Crowns, befides the Thirds, to which they are obliged in time of War. *Its Revenues.*

This State, for a need, can raife fifty thoufand Men. *Its Strength.*

He that defires to know the Hiftory of *Milan*, let him read *Corio* of the Hiftory of *Milan*, *Ripamontius*, *Scipio Barbono* of the Lives of the Dukes of *Milan*, and *Paola Morigi*. *Its Hiftorians.*

Having thus feen *Milan* in fix days time, we took Horfe for *Bologna*, fix days Journey from hence, and paffed through *Marignano, Lodi, Piarenza, Parma, Regio, Modena, Fort Urbano*, and fo to *Bologna*; of each I will fay fomething.

Marignano is a little Town about ten miles diftant from *Milan*, and from thence to *Lodi* the way is moft pleafant, and level as an Alley. Near to this Town *Francis* the Firft of *France* fought with the *Swiffers* a famous Battel, and killed 16000 of them, and took *Ludovicus Sforza* the Duke of *Milan*, who thought to have efcaped in the *Swiffers* Clothes, but was difcover'd. *Marignano.*

Lodi is a good Town, and Frontier upon the *Venetians*; the River *Adda* runs under its Walls. It's call'd *Lodi* either becaufe it's built upon the Ruins, or near to old *Lodi*, which was call'd *Laus Pompeia*, becaufe *Pompey* had reftor'd it. This Town is famous for excellent Neats Tongues, and Cheefes as big as Millftones. A Gentleman of this Town caus'd four Cheefes *Lodi.*

Cheefes to be made, each one weighing 500 pound weight. The People here mow their Hay three times a year, and I am afraid they are polled as often with Taxes.

Piacenza. *Piacenza,* or *Pleafance,* deferves its name, by reafon of its fweet fituation in a rich Country near the *Po* and *Trebia,* two great Rivers. Near the laft of which *Hannibal* overcame *Sempronius* the *Roman* Conful. The Country round about this Town is very rich in Pafturage; hence their excellent Cheefes and rare Cream. It aboundeth alfo in Salt-pits, which afford no fmall profit. This Town belongs to the Duke of *Parma.*

its Rarities. The beft things to be feen here, are, the *Equeftris Statua* of the fecond *Alexander the Great,* or the firft *Alexander of Parma.* It's in Brafs in the Market-place. The old Fountain made by *Auguftus Cæfar;* the rare Picture of *Raphael's* hand, in the *Benedictins* Church, behind the high Altar; the Churches of the *Dominicans,* and *Canon Regulars,* are no contemptible ones.

A piece of Thrift. I obferved in this Town a notable piece of Thriftinefs ufed by the Gentlewomen, who make no fcruple to be carried to their Country Houfes near the Town in Coaches drawn by two Cows yoked together; thefe will carry the *Signora* a pretty round trot under her *Villa;* they afford her alfo a dish of their Milk, and after collation, bring her home again at night, without fpending a penny.

Its Hiftory. He that defires to know more of *Piacenza,* let him read *Umberto Loccati.*

Part I. A Voyage to ITALY.

Of *Piacenza*, where *Cornelius Muffo*, Bishop of *Bitonti*, a great preacher, and a *Trent* Father; as also *Ferrante Pallavicini*.

Parma belongs also to the Duke of *Parma*, of the House of *Farnese*. This Dutchy was given to *Pier Luigi Farnese*, by *Paulus* III, upon condition it should hold of the Pope, and pay him yearly ten thousand Crowns; it's worth to the Duke two hundred thousand Crowns. This Town of *Parma* is three miles in compass, hath the River *Parma* running thro' it, over which is built a handsom Stone Bridge. The Country round about the Town is most fertile, and begets such credit to the Cheeses, that *Parmesan* Cheeses are famous over all the World. *Parma.*

The chief things to be seen in *Parma*, are these; the Duke's Palace, with the Gardens, Fountains, wild Beasts, the admirable Theatre to exhibit *Opera's* in; the exquisite Coaches of the Duke, one whereof is all of beaten Silver, with the Seats and Curtains embroider'd with Gold and Silver; another so well gilt and adorn'd, that it's almost as rich as the former. Lastly, the Stables, where I saw Horses suitable both in strength and beauty to the foresaid Coaches. *The Duke's Palace.*

Then I went to the *Dome*, whose Cupola was painted by the rare hand of *Coreggio*. *The Domo.*

Lastly, to the *Capuchins*, in whose Church lies buried my noble Hero *Alexander Farnese*, Duke of *Parma*, whom I cannot meet in this my Voyage without a Complement. He was the *third Duke* of *Parma*, but the *tenth Worthy*. Indeed his leaping the first Man into the *Turks* Galleys, in the Battel of *Lepanto*, with Sword *The Capuchins. Alexander Farnese.*

in

in hand, and in the eighteenth year only of his age, was such a Prognostick of his future worth, his reducing *Flanders* again, with the prodigious Actions done by him at the taking of *Antwerp*, was such a making good of the Prognostick; and his coming into *France* in his Slippers and Sedan, to succour *Rouen*, besieg'd by *Henry* IV, was such a crowning of all his other Actions, that his History begets belief to *Quintus Curtius*, and makes Men believe, that *Alexander*'s can do any thing.

Some Criticks hold Quintus Curtius to be a Romance.

The *Revenues* of this Prince are said to be *Six hundred thousand Crowns* a year. He is now of the French Faction, and in all his Territories he can raise 28000 Men.

The Duke's Revenues. His Interest.

Here is an Academy of Wits, call'd the *Innominati*, as they that had rather be wise than be talked of, or famed for such.

His Forces. The Academy of Wits.

This Town hath furnish'd *Italy* with two excellent Painters, *Coreggio* and *Parmigiano*.

He that would know the particular History of *Parma*, let him read *Bonaventura Arrighi*.

Its History.

From *Parma* we went to *Regio*, a Town belonging to the Duke of *Modena*; here is a neat Cathedral Church, of which Church S. *Prosper* was Bishop. Of this Town were these three learned men, *Guido Pancirola*, Cardinal *Tosco*, and snarling *Castelvetro*.

Regio.

Modena is the Town where the Duke keeps his Court. It's a handsome Town, and by its high Steeple shews it self to Travellers long before they come to it. It hath also a strong Citadel, which lying flat and even with the Town, sheweth the Town, that indeed it can be even with it whensoever it shall rebel.

Modena.

The

Part I.   A Voyage to ITALY.   93

The Palace of the Duke hath some Rooms in it as neat, and rich, as any I saw in *Italy*, witness those Chambers hung round with the Pictures of those of his Family, and Wainscoted with great *Looking-Glasses* and rich guilding.

This Duke is of the Family of *Este*, but not of the true Line: Wherefore for want of lawful Heirs Male, *Ferrara* and *Commachio* fell to the Church in *Clement* the VIII's time, and remain there ever since. *The Family of Este.*

Of the true House of *Este*, was the brave Countess *Matilda* the *Dry-Nurse*, as I may say, of the *Roman Church*. For it was she defended *Gregory* the VII. against the *Emperor Henry* the VI. and brought him to acknowledge his fault, and cry the *Pope* mercy. It was she also that by Will and *Testament* left the *Pope Parma*, *Regio*, *Mantua*, and *Ferrara*. Hence *Urban* the VIII. out of gratitude to this Princess, caused her Statue and Tomb to be set up in St. *Peter's* Church in *Rome*. The Will and Testament of this Princess are kept in *Lucca* to this day. *Countess Matilda.*

Hard by *Modena* was fought the famous Battle where *Hirtius* and *Pansa* being Consuls, the Senate lost in them its Authority. *The last true Consuls.*

Of *Modena* were these Famous Men in learning, Cardinal *Sadoletus*, *Carolus Sigonius*, and *Gabriel Falopius*. *Its Learned Men.*

In *Modena* are made the best Visards for Masquerades; and it's no small profit which they draw from this foolish Commodity, seeing *Stultorum plena sunt omnia*.

The Revenues of this Duke are Three hundred thousand Crowns a year: and he is now of the *French* Faction. He can raise 30000 Men. *The Duke's Revenues. His Interest.*

From

His Forces Fort Urban.

From thence passing the River we came soon to Fort *Urban*, a Cittadal most regularly built by the Command of Pope *Urban* the VIII. from whom it's called. It's so strong, that it is not afraid to stand night and day alone in the fields, and upon the *Frontiers* of the Pope's Estate.

Castel Franco.

Passing from hence through *Castel Franco*, antiently called *Forum Gallorum*, we arrived betimes at *Bologna*.

Bologna.

Bologna is one of the greatest Towns of *Italy*, and one of the handsomest. It's the second of the Pope's Dominions; and the chief University of *Italy* for Law. Hence the *Jurists* say it is, *Musarum domus, atque omnis nutricula Juris*, and the very common Coin of the Country tells you that *Bononia docet*.

It's named by the Common Proverb, *Bologna la grassa:* because of the fertil Soyl in which it stands, to wit, in the very end of *Lombardy*; and the many Springs which humect it from the *Apennine Hills*, at whose feet it stands.

This Country was antiently called *Felsina*, *Gallia Cisalpina*, *Gallia Togata*, to distinguish it from *Gallia Braccata*, the Country in *France* near *Narbonne*, and from *Gallia Comata*, the Country in *France* called *La Guienne*. In middling Ages it was called *Romagnola*, because *Bologna*, *Ravenna*, *Cesena*, *Forli*, *Faenza*, and *Imola* stood constant to the City of *Rome* against the *Lombards* for a long time.

The Town it self.

As for the Town of *Bologna* now, it's excellently well built; and for the most part upon Arches, like the *Covent-Garden* in *London*; only the Pillars are round. These *Arches* bring great conveniency to the Inhabitants, who can walk all

Part I.   A Voyage to ITALY.   95

all the Town over *cool* and *dry*, even in *July*
and *January*. It's five miles in compass, and an
excellent Summer Town, were it not that the
Air is not altogether so pure, and the Wines
heating. It's groverned by a *Legat a Latere*,
sent hither by the Pope, and in change, it sends *Its Go-*
and Embassador to *Rome* to reside there: so *vernment.*
that *Bologna* is treated by *Rome* rather like a
Sister, than a *Subject*: and deservedly, seeing *Its Privi-*
Bologna fell not to the *Church* any other way but *leges.*
by her free giving her self to the *Pope*, reserving
only to her self some particular Privileges; as
power to send Embassadors to *Rome*; and that
if any Townsman kill another, and can but e-
scape away, his goods cannot be confiscated.

I staid six days here, in which time I saw
these things.   *The Domi-*
    1. The *Dominicans Church* and *Convent*. In *nicans*
the Church, I saw the *Tomb* of S. *Dominick* Foun- *Church.*
der of that *Order*. It's all of *White Marble* cut
with curious Figures relating to his Life. In
this Church is kept a Famous Manuscript, to wit
the Bible it self written in Parchment by *Esdras*
himself, saith *Leandro Alberto*, the *Cambden* of
Italy, and a *Friar* of this Convent. They shew
you also here a curious Lamp sent to St. *Domi-*
nick's Tomb by the new converted *Indians*. It's
of a most rare Workmanship. Behind the *high*
Altar stands the *Quire*, so famous for the *Seats*,
which are of rare *Mosaick* work of Coloured
Wood, inlaid into Pictures representing the
Old and *New Testaments*, and all wrought by one
Lay Brother called *Fra. Damiano di Bergamo*.
This kind of *Mosaick Work* in Wood was anti-
ently (saith *Vasari*) called *Tarsia*, and in this
                                                            kind

96 A Voyage to ITALY. Part I.

kind of Work *Brunelleschi* and *Maiano* did good things in *Florence*. But *John Veronese* improved it much afterwards by boiling Wood into several colours, and then inlaying it into what Postures and Figures he pleased. This *Quire* is shewn to Strangers as a rare thing; and worthily, since the Emperor *Charles* the V. had the curiosity to see it, and with the point of his Dagger to try whether it was inlaid, or only painted; and the piece which he picked out with his Dagger, was never put in again for a Memorandum. In this Church, as also in the Chapterhouse and Cloister of this Convent, lie buried many Readers of the Law, who having lived here by the Law, died here also by the Law of Nature.

The Dominicans Convent. 2. The Convent here is one of the fairest in *Europe*, in which 150 Friars constantly live and study. The little Chapel, which was once S. *Dominick's Chamber*; the vast *Dormitory*; the fair *Library*; the great *Refectory*, and curious *Celler* are shewn courteously to Strangers.

The Body Beata Catherina. 3. The Nunnery of *Corpus Christi*. It's of S. *Clare's Order*, and famous for the Body of *Beata Catherina di Bologna* a most holy Nun of this Order and Convent. I saw her Body sitting straight up in a Chair, in her Religious Habit: She holds her Rules in her right hand; and we see her Face and Feet plainly, but those black and dried up.

The Corso. 4. From hence I went on to the Town Gate, a little out of which Gate lies a fair Street where they make the Corso of Coaches in Summer Evenings.

Part I. A Voyage to ITALY. 97

5. Turning from hence on the left hand, I *S. Michael* went to S. *Michael* in *Bosco* a stately Monastery *in Bosco.* of *Olivetan Fathers*; standing upon a high Hill. From this Hill I had a perfect view of *Bologna* under me, and of all the Country about it: which being level and strowed with a world of white Houses and *Villa*'s, looked like a Sea loaden with Ships under sail. Entering into this Monastery, I saw the Oval Court painted by several Prime Masters, of which *Guido Rheni* of *Bologna* was one. Then mounting up to the Dormitory, I found it to be one of the fairest I had ever seen.

6. The Monastery, or Convent of the *Fran-* *Other state-* *ciscans*, with the rare row of Pillars, and Por- *ly Monaste-* tico towards the Street, the excellent Cloisters, *ries.* and the curious Cellar.

7. The Monastery of St. *Salvatore* with its two vast Courts or double Cloister built upon Galleries above, it's a noble Building.

8. The Monastery of the *Servits*, that of the *Augustins*, and that of the *Carmalites*, are all of them such stately Buildings, that I may boldly say, that no Town in *Europe* is comparable to *Bologna* for fair Monasteries.

9. Then I visited *San Petronio*, standing in *S. Petro-* the end of the great Piazza. of which Church *nio's* *Leandro Albarto* writ a hundred years ago, that *Church.* he thought it would not be ended but with the World. And I am half of his opinion: for when I passed that way last, I found the Scafolds yet standing, which I had found there one and twenty years before; and yet in all my five Voyages into *Italy*, I found them always knocking and making as much noise and
H dust

duſt, as if this Church ſhould be finiſhed within half a year, when as yet half of it is only finiſhed. In this Church *Charles* the V. was crowned Emperor by *Clement* the VII.

The Domo. 10. The *Domo*, which is not yet half finiſhed neither: yet that part which is finiſhed promiſeth fair for the reſt.

Other Churches. 11. The New Church of St. *Paul* hath a curious High Altar. In the Church of St. *Giovanni in Morte* is the rare Picture of St. *Cecily* of the hand of *Raphael Urbin*. The Jeſuits Church, the Church of St. *Stephen*, and that of the *Paſſion*, deſerve to be ſeen.

The Legats Palace. 12. After the Churches and Monaſteries, we went on with viſiting the reſt of the Town, and ſaw the Palace of the Popes Legate: in this Palace I ſaw the rare Cabinet and Study of *Aldrovandus*, to whom *Pliny* the Second if he were now alive, would but be *Pliny* the Sixth, for he hath printed ſix great Volumes of the nature of things, each Volume being as big as all *Pliny*'s

Aldrovandus his Study and Cabinet. Works. They ſhewed me here two or three hundred Manuſcripts, all of this Mans own hand-writing, and all of them Notes out of the beſt Authors; out of which Notes he compiled his ſix great Volumes which are now in print. Seeing theſe Manuſcripts, I asked whether the Man had lived three hundred years, or no, as it's ſaid *Joannes de Temporibus* in *Charles* the *Great*'s time did: but it was anſwered me, that he lived only fourſcore and three: a ſhort age for ſuch a long Work: but it ſheweth us how far a Man may travel in Sciences in his Life time if he riſe early and ſpur on all his Life time with obſtinate Labour. Certainly had he

wrote

Part I. *A Voyage to* ITALY. 99

wrote before *Solomon*, that wife Man would
have changed his saying, and inftead of fend-
ing the flothful Man to learn of the *Pifmire*
how to labour, he would have fent him to
Aldrovandus his Study and Example: *Vade ad
Aldrovandum piger.*

13. The Great Schools here where the Do- *The Schools*
ctors of the Univerfity read, are ftately both
within and without.

14. The *Spanifh College* founded here by no- *The Spa-*
ble *Cardinal Albernozzo*, deferves to be taken *nifh Col-*
notice of. It's well built with a handfome *lege.*
Church and five Priefts to ferve it. The intention of his College is to furnifh all the
King of *Spains* Dominions in *Italy* with able
Magiftrates and Officers of Juftice. None can
live in it but natural *Spaniards* (except the
Chaplains,) and thofe *Spaniards* muft be Doctors of the Law before they can be admitted
here ; they only learn the language and Cu-
ftoms of the Countries, and perfect themfelves
in the ftudy of the Law, that they may be fit
to fill up the firft vacant places of Judicature
that fall either in the State of *Milan*, in the
Kingdom of *Naples*, or in *Sicily*. They have
a revenue of twelve thoufand Crowns a year.
They keep two Coaches, live very nobly, and
lodge all *Spanifh Embaffadors, Cardinals* and
Prelates of their Nation that pafs this way. In
the College you fee the Pictures of many great
Statefmen and Cardinals and others who have
been of this College: but no Picture pleafed
me like that of their brave Founder, Noble
Cardinal *Albernozzo*, which is in the Church,

H 2   and

and reprefenting him in the fame pofture he was in, when he recovered all the Pope's State in *Italy*, unto the Pope then at *Avignon*; of which I have fpoken fufficiently above in defcribing *Avignon*.

The two Towers.

15. The two *Towers* here in the midft of the Town, the one very high and ftreight, called *De gli Afinelli*; the other low and bending, called, *La Cariffenda*. They would make us believe that this bending *Tower* was made crooked a-purpofe; and it's ftrange to fee how moft Men make it their bufinefs rather to *fee* this low crooked Tower, than the other, which is both higher and ftreighter. But there's no Myftery to make things ill, and to mifs of our aims; and I rather think the *Cariffenda* or low Tower went not up higher, becaufe the Architect perceiv'd it went up awry. But we ftrangers admire every thing in ftrange Countries, and that makes that none admire us; upon which occafion I would wifh my young Traveller never to admire any thing in outward fhew, but to look curioufly at every thing, with crying out, *O che Bela Cofa!* This will get him and his Nation far more honour, for *Admiration* is but the Daughter of *Ignorance*; and *Magnanimus* (faith *Ariftotle*) *nihil admiratur*.

The Houfes in Bologna

16. Then the *Houfes* here, which are generally well built, and in Summer-time fetting open their Doors and Gates towards the Street, you may look quite through their Courts, Entries, Porches, Houfes, and a huge way into their Gardens, which, even from thence, will falute your Eye with a fair profpect of Fountains, and frefh Verdure; and your Nofe too with de-

delicate smells of Jesomin and Orange flowers. Now the best Palaces here are those of *Malvezzi, Campeggi, Pepoli, Fachinetti, Cespi,* and others.

17. These fine Houses are full also of Nobility, and I remember to have seen here at a *Corso di Paglio* upon *Midsummer-day*, the long great Street lined quite through with Coaches on both sides, and those Coaches double lin'd with Ladies and Cavaliers of *Garbo.* Indeed it would be pity that such a stately Town as *Bologna* should, like *Leyden* in *Holland,* be full only of *Houses* and *Boren.* *The Nobility.*

18. Their *Traffick* here consisteth much in Silks, Velvets, Olives, Leather-bottles, Gellies, Washballs, and little Dogs for Ladies, which here are so little, that the Ladies carrying them in their Muffs, have place enough for their Hands too. *The Traffick*

19. Their Markets here are also well furnish'd with all Provisions; witness their *Salsicci* only, which are a *Regalo* for a Prince. *The Marketts.*

20. But that you may not think them better fed than taught; they have erected here an Academy of *Wits,* called *Gli Otiosi,* or *Idlemen, per antiphrasin,* because they are not idle. It's this Academy (I believe) which hath helpt to set out three excellent modern Writers of this Town, Cardinal *Bentivoglio,* the Marquiss of *Malvezzi* and *John Baptista Manzini*; the first, a *Titus Livius*; the second, a *Lucius Florus*; and the third, a *Marcus Tullius* of his time. To whom I may add *Leandro Alberti,* the *Camden* of *Italy.* *The Academy of Wits.* *The Learned Men.*

H 3   21. He

102   A Voyage to ITALY.   Part I.

The Histo- 21. He that desires to know the particular
rians. History of *Bologna*, let him read *Bartholomeo*, *Galeotti*, and *Giovanni Garzo*, where he shall find how *Bologna* suffer'd much anciently by the two opposite Factions of the *Lambartazzi* and the *Ceremei*. But now they enjoy quiet and repose under the Pope.

Remember the Bolet- tina, Tra- veller. Having thus seen *Bologna*, and being arm'd with a *Bolettina di Sanita*, taken here, to make us be let pass into the State of *Florence*, we steer-ed on Horseback towards *Florence*, and reach'd it in two days, the first days Journey by *Piano- ra, Loiano, Scargo, L'Azino, Pietra Mala*, and over

The Apen- nine Hills. the *Apennines*, was long and tedious enough, till the night came, at which time we were much recreated with the sight of a Fire which appea-red some two miles off, in the side of a Moun-tain on our left hand. This Fire appears here frequently, especially in cloudy weather; and it appear'd to me for an hour together as I rode along, to be still of the same bigness, and of the same glowy colour (Furnace like) and of a per-fect round form, and not pyramidial, as other flames are: the Country People here call this Fire, *La Bocca d' Inferno, Hell's Mouth*; and I

Tertul. l. de Peni- tent. c. 12. know not why they may not as well call this Fire so, as *Tertullian* calls *Vesuvius* and *Ætna* (two *burning Mountains*) *Fumariola Inferni, Hell's Chim- neys*. Taken in fine, with this fixed Meteor, we forgot the tediousness of the way, and came

Fiorenzuo- la. to *Fiorenzuola*; the next morning passing by *Scarperia* and *Il Ponte*, we arriv'd betimes at *Flo-rence*.

I con-

Part I. A Voyage to ITALY.

I confess I stirred not out of my Inn that night, because *Fair Florence* (as the Proverb calls her) is not to be seen in foul Linnen and Riding-boots; but rising betimes the next Morning, I made my Eyes survey such Beauty, as even Princes Eyes might feast upon. *My arrival at Florence.*

But before I come to the particulars of what I saw in *Florence*, I will consider it in great, and then come to the retail of it.

Divers good Authors are of opinion that this Town was first built by *Sylla*'s Soldiers, to whom he had given this Soyl, for their services done him in his Civil Wars. They built it near the Current of two Rivers (*Arno* and *Munio*) and from thence it was called at first *Fluentia* (as *Coblentz* in *Germany*, from the meeting of Rivers, is called *Confluentia*. Afterwards by the Inhabitants it was called *Florentia*, by reason of the fruitful soyl which made it flourish with all delicacies; as also for the flourishing Wits of the Inhabitants, who were so famous antiently in point of Wit, that the very *Romans* used to send their Children first into *Tuscany*, to be bred in *Learning* and *Religion*, and then into *Greece*, to learn *Greek* and *Philosophy*. *Florence.*

I spent a month in this Town, and the things I observed most were these:

1. The Chapel of St. *Laurence*, which is the neatest thing that ever eye beheld. All the inside of it is to be over-crusted with *Jasper Stones*, of several Colours and Countries, with other rich Stones, all above Marble, and all so neatly polished and shining, [that the Art here exceeds the Materials. This Chapel is round, and round about are to be fixed within *The Chapel of Saint Laurence.*

H 4 the

the Walls, as high as a Man can reach, the Tombs of all he great Dukes of *Florence*, in a moſt gallant manner, and of moſt exquiſite poliſhed Stones, with a great Cuſhion of ſome richer Stone, and a Ducal Crown of Precious Stones repoſing upon that Cuſhion. Over theſe *Tombs* the Statues of all the Great Dukes, at full length, and in their Ducal Habits, all of Braſs guilt, are to be placed in *Niches* round about the Chapel. The Roof is to be vaulted all over with an over-cruſting of *Lapis Lazuli* (a blue precious Stone with veins of Gold in it) which will make it look like Heaven it ſelf. Between each Tomb are inlaid in the Walls, the Arms, or Scutchions of the ſeveral Towns of the Great Dukes Dominions, all blazoned according to their ſeveral Colours in Heraldry by ſeveral precious Stones which compoſe them: and theſe are not made in little, but are fair great Scutchions made purpoſely of a large ſize for to fill up the void places between the *Tomb*: the Towns are theſe *Florence, Siena, Piſa, Livorno, Volterra, Arezzo, Piſtoia, Cortona, Monte Pal-ciano*, &c. which contributed (I ſuppoſe) ſomething each of them to this Coſtly Fabrick. In fine, this Chapel is ſo rich within with its own ſhining bare Walls, that it ſcorns all Hangings, Painting, Gilding, Moſaick Work, and ſuch like helpers off of bare Walls, becauſe it can find nothing richer and handſomer than its own precious Walls. It's now above threeſcore years ſince it was begun, and there are ordinarily threeſcore Men at work daily here, and yet there's only the Tomb of *Ferdinand* the Second, perfectly finiſhed. The very Cuſhion which lieth upon his Tomb, coſt threeſcore thouſand Crowns, by which you may gueſs at the reſt. Indeed theſe ſtately Tombs make almoſt death it ſelf look lovely, and dead mens aſhes grown proud again. As for the Altar and Tabernacle of this Chapel, I will ſpeak of them by and by, when I will deſcribe the Gallery of the Great Duke, where they are kept till the Chapel be finiſhed.

2. The Church of St. *Laurence*, to which be- *The Church* longs the Chapel, or rather to which this Cha- *of St. Lau-* pel belongs; is a very handſome Church de- *renzo.* ſigned by *Brunelleſchi* himſelf. The things that grace this Church are the neat double-row of round Pillars which hold up the Roof of this Fabrick. The Picture over the Quire painted in the Roof, repreſenting the general Judgment. It's a bold piece, and of *Ponturno*: The two *Brazen Pulpits* wrought into Hiſtories by rare *Donatello*: The curious deſigned Picture of S. *Anne* and our Bleſſed Lady, in *chiaro è oſcuro*, by *Fra. Bartolomeo*, commonly called *Del Frate*, is ſo well a deſigned Piece, that a Duke of *Mantua* having ſeen it, offered to buy it at any rate, but was refuſed. The new Sacriſty made to ſerve the fine Chapel deſcribed above) deſerves to be carefully viſited, becauſe of the Bodies of the Princes of the Family of *Medices*, which are depoſited here, till the Chapel mentioned above be finiſhed. In this new Sacriſty alſo are ſeen the four Statues made by *Michael Angelo*, repreſenting the *Day*, the *Night*, *Aurora*, and the *Evening*; the four parts which compoſe Time, by which all Men are brought to their Graves: That which re-
preſents

presents *Night* is a rare Statue, and hugely cryed up by all Sculptors and Virtuosi. See also in the Wall of the old Sacrifty the neat *Tomb* of *John* and *Peter Medices*, Sons of *Cosmus*, surnamed *Peter Patrie*: It's the work of *Andrea Varockio*. In the midst of this Church before the High Altar, lies buried *Cosmus Peter Petrie*, the raiser of the *Medicean* Family. In the Cloifter joyning to this Church, is erected the Statue of *Paulus Jovius* the Historian; and near to this Statue you mount up a pair of stairs to the rare Library of Manuscripts, called *Bibliotheca Laurentiana*, the Catalogue of whose Books is Printed at *Amsterdam* Anno 1622. in *Octavo*.

The Library.

3. The Gallery of the old Palace. This is that Gallery so famous, and so freequently visited by all Strangers: At your entrance into this Gallery you see a vast long Room made like an L: on the left hand of this Gallery, there runs a perpetual glass Window; on the other side are set a row of Pictures in great, of those of the *Medicean* Family: under the Windows, and also under the said Pictures stand a row of curious *Marble Statues*, antient ones all, and of prime hands. Over the said Windows and Pictures runs a close row of less Pictures, representing to the Life, the most famous Men of Latter times for Learning and Arms; the Soldiers being on the right hand, and the Scholars on the left. The Statues aforesaid are well nigh a hundred in all, but all rare ones: Some whereof I yet remember, and they are these: that of *Leda*, of *Diana*, of *Bacchus*, of *Hercules*, of the *Gladiator* standing on his Guard,

The great Dukes Gallery.

Part I. A Voyage to ITALY. 107

Guard, of *Scipio Africanus* in Brass, shewing the ancient Habit and Dress of the old *Romans*, far different from our modes, that of a little young youth in Brass, with his Sword in his hand, that of a little Boy sleeping upon a Touchstone, the Head of *Cicero* in Marble, that of *Seneca*, the Head of *Michael Angelo Bonarota* in Brass of his own hand making: in fine, the Head of *Brutus*, one of *Cæsar*'s Murderers. It was begun in Marble by *Michael Angelo*, but informidly; and so left by him: If you will know the reason why he finished it not, read the distich written in Brass, under this Head by the said sculptor himself, thus:

 M. *Dum Bruti effigiem Sculptor* A.
  de marmore ducit,
 B. *In mentem sceleris Venit, &* F.
  abstinuit.

The four Corner letters signifying that *Michael Angelus Bonarota Fecit.* Among the Pictures I took particular notice of these Soldiers, of *Hannibal* that frighted *Rome*, of *Scipio* that took *Carthage* and vanquished *Hannibal*, of *Pyrrhus* that made the *Romans* glad to make Peace with him, of *Scanderbeg* that made the great *Turk* afraid to fight with him, of *Venerius* that helpt to win the Battle of *Lepanta*, of *Alexander Farnese* that never lost Battle, of *Cortesius* that found out new Countries, of *Magellanus* that found out new Seas, of *Andrea d' Oria* who beat the *French* by Sea, of *Gustom de Foix* who had beat the *Spaniards* by Land, if he had but known how to use his Victory, of the Duke of *Alva*

Pictures of Famous Soldiers.

who

who only lamented dying, that he had never fought a pitch'd Battle with the *Turks*, of *Anne de Montmorancy*, who died in a pitch'd Battel against the *Hugnots*, of *Ecclino* the *Panduan Tyrant*, of whom no Man can speak any good, of *Casiratio*, of whom no Man can speak any ill; with a world of other brave *Heroes*, with whose true looks I was very glad to be acquainted.

Pictures of learned Men.
Among the Pictures of the learned Men, I took particular notice of these *Italians*, to wit, *Petrarch*, *Ariosto*, *Joannes Casa*, *Poggio*, *Macchiavel*, *Guicciardin*, *Paulo Jovio*, *Sannazario*, *Bocaccio*, *Platina*, *Brunellefchi*, *Michael Angelo*, *Raphel Urbin*, *Columbus*, *Americus*, and *Galileo*, with many others too long to relate, and too many to be remembred. Having thus gazed our fill at these Statues and Pictures, and by particular taking notice of them, complimented the great Worthies they represent, we were let into the great Cabinets, or Chambers which joyn upon this Gallery.

The Armory.
First, we saw the Armory, that is, three or four great Chambers full of exotick curiosities: as the Habits of two *Indian Kings* made of Parrats Feathers sowed together; the Habits of some Janisaries in *Turkey*, of red Velvet set thick with little Nails of gold, which they can take out and dress up other suits with; the habit of the King of *China*; the skin of a Horse pasted upon a Wooden Horse, the Mane of which Horse is kept there in a Box all at length, and it is above five Ells long: This Horse had been sent to the Great Duke by the Duke of *Lorain*. Then we were shown *Hannibal*'s Helmet; the

Helmet

Helmet of *Charles* the V. the Sword of *Henry* the IV. of *France*, a curious Helmet thin and light, and yet of Musket proof, a huge heavy Helmet and Sword of one of the old *Paladins* of *France*; the true Sword of *Scanderbeg*, a world of Cimetars, *Scabbards, Caps, Saddles,* and other *Turkish* Furniture set thick with *Turquoises* in Gold; a great Gun, whose thick Barrel is of pure Gold, and yet as long as an ordinary fowling piece, and as heavy as a strong Man can well level with: It's valued at 1500 Pistols, and shoots twice as far as another Gun of Iron doth, but kills (I believe) with the same pain that others do, though with a little more honour. Here is a great Pistol of Gold. Then the *buona notte*, or Set of Pistols, (five Pistol Barrels set together in an Iron Frame) to put into your Hat, and to be all shot off at once from thence, as you seem to salute your Enemy, and bid him Good night. The Pistole with eighteen Barrels in it, all to be shot off at once, and scattering desperately about a Room, six little Cannons set in Star-wise. The little *Brass Cannon* which may be taken in pieces presently, and set together as soon, and so be carried easily into any Steeple, or Tower: such Cannons as these might easily be carried in deep Countries, and over high Mountains, every Soldier carrying a Piece. The Statue in Brass of the *King of Spain, Philip the Fourth* on Horseback, just of the brightness of that of Gold which the Great Duke sent to the said King of *Spain* for a Present: It was made by rare *John di Bologna.* Then I saw the Armour for Horse and Man of two Kings of *Persia.* The Armour of the *Great Duke Ferdinad,* a goodly ly Man. The King of *Sweede*'s Cornet taken in *Germany* in a Battle. The *Buckler* with the *Medusa*'s Head on it, painted by *Michael Angelo*. A *Turkish Bell* to ring in time of Battle. A Horn ufed in *Turkey* to call Men to their Mofques in ftead of *Bells*, as we have. The head of a Halbard ringing like a Bell. A Halbard to fold up in three, and to carry under your Cloak privately. A *Staff of white Cane*, in which are curioufly engraven in black, the Hiftories of the *Apocalypfe*. It was the Duke of *Urbin*'s. In fine, the *Loadftone* holding up threefcore pound weight of Iron ; and holding one Key to another, for a matter of five or fix Keys.

The 1. *Cabinet*. After the Armory, we were let into the five Cabinets full of precious Jewels, Pictures, and other rare curiofities. In the firft Cabinet I was fhown a curious Candleftick to hang up in the middle of a Room, with feveral Branches fpreading from it, and all of yellow *Amber*, including within it a world of little figures of white Marble or Wax, neatly cut in little, and appearing through the tranfparent yellow Amber : This Candleftick was given by the Dutchefs of *Lunenburg*, to the Duke of *Saxony*, and by him to Prince *Matthias* Brother to this Great Duke of *Florence*. In the fame Cabinet, I faw a Table of polifhed ftones of feveral colours and luftre, inlaid into Birds and Flowers. The head of *Tiberius Cefar* in one Turkey ftone, as big as a Ducks egg, and of an ineftimable value. A curious Cabinet, or two of *Ivory Cups*, brought out of *Germany* by Prince *Matthias*. In the fame Cabinet I faw the picture of Cardinal *Bembo* in a neat *Mofaick* work ; and another piece of
divers

Part I. *A Voyage to* ITALY.   111

divers Birds in Mosaik also, rarely done by *Marcellus Provincialis*. I saw also there divers little old Pagan Idols in Iron and Brass, a design of *Raphael's* own hand; and some good Pictures.

In the second Cabinet I saw two great *Globes*, which were made in this Room, being too great ever to be carried out, or brought into it by the Door. I saw also here a curious Table of polish'd stones, representing a Town in *Bohemia*, with divers Pictures of Men, Horses, and Landskips: where there is a Tree represented most naturally, because it is represented by the very Wood of a *Tree Petrified* into stone, and looking like Wood as it was; and shining like polished stone, as it now is. The Statues, or *Busto's* of three or four of the Great Dukes, in *Porphyry*. A curious looking Glass over the inside of the Door, which placed directly over the Picture of a Man, contracts into it the Picture of a Woman that Man's Wife) which you see plainly in it; drawing thus *Eve* out of *Adam* again by a curious reflexion. *The 2. Cabinet.*

In the third Cabinet I was shown a curious Table of polished Stones, representing perfectly the Town and Haven of *Legorne*, A great Cabinet of *Ebony* beset with precious Stones on the outside, and with the History of the Holy *Scriptures* curiously expressed in miniature in several little Squares of rich Stones set here and there. In the top of it there is a *German Clock*, now out of order, and no Man dare mend it. Within this great *Cabinet* I saw the *passion of our Saviour* curiously cut by *Michael Angelo* in Ivory (say they) but I believe it's in white Wax. There *The 3. Cabinet.*

is

is also in it the figures of our Saviour and his twelve Apostles in yellow Amber, with their Heads in white Amber: All these several pieces are not seen at once, but come up into sight one after another, as the Man turns them.

This *Ebony Cabinet* was sent to the *Great Duke* by the Duke of *Bavaria*, and it's valued at fourscore thousand Crowns : I believe, if it were to be sold, it would not yield forty thousand Crowns ; but it's handsome, saith *Seneca*, for those that receive courtesies, to value them high. Here are also some Pictures of great value, as the *Adam* and *Eve* of the hand of *Alberto Durero*; an Original piece, valued at 1500 Crowns. An original *Venus* of *Titian*, that in the *Poggio Imperiale* here (of which below) looking but like a good copy of this. Here are also several *Persian* Chairs, and other good Originals of prime Hands.

The 4th. Cabinet. In the 4th Cabinet, called *Il Tribuno* we saw more riches than in all the others. This *Tribuno* is a great Room built round with a *Cupola*, whose Vault is painted with a deep sanguin red, set full with the shells of Mother of Pearl. The Walls of this Room are hung with green Silk, and loaden with excellent Pictures of the prime Masters of the World, *Titian*, *Raphael*, *Andrea del Sarto*, *Vinci*, *Hans Holbain*, *Vandike* and others. The St. *John Baptist* is of *Raphael*'s hand; as is also that of *Leo* the X. with two Cardinals, *Julio Medici*, and Cardinal *Rossi* behind him. The Picture of *Southwel*, Privy Counseller to *Henry* the VIII. is of the hand of rare *Hans Holbain*: The Picture of our Lady with our Saviour in her Arms, is of the hand of *Andrea del Sarto*.

The

Part I. A Voyage to ITALY.

The Picture of Cardinal *Bentivoglio* sitting in a Chair, is of the hand of *Vandike*. There is also a rare Picture in *miniature* of *GiulioGlorio*'s hand, and three fair pieces in *miniature* of an *Augustin Friar* yet living, and a Man of great esteem, having taken the right course to be famous, that is, to make but few pieces, but these finished with all the patience which *miniature* requires. In this *Tribuno* I saw also the famous Nail, half Gold, half Iron; made by the famous *Alchymist Thurnheuser*. They shewed me also a great Lump of Gold, not yet stamped into Coyn; two shells of Mother *of Pearl* with their two *Pearls* still sticking to them, and just as they grow: The *Pearls* are rich *Pearls* and round. The two pieces of Emerauld-Rock, the one scarce formed yet into perfect Emerauld, but only begun: the other quite finished and green. Then two close Cupboards within the Walls of this Room, in which I saw a world of curious Cups and Vases of Cryftal, *Agate, Lapis, Lazuli*, and other such curious, but brittle matter, yet of rare Fabrick and Shape: they value them at two hundred thousand Crowns. The *Unicorns Horn*, and the Alabaster Pillar, are not to be forgotten. The great *Cabinet* of *Ebony* standing at the further end of this *Tribuno*, full of ancient Medals of Gold, Silver and Brass, of the ancient Consuls and Emperours, all digested into their several Series; and yet this *Cabinet* is almost as rich without, as it contains riches within; being set without with precious stones, of a vast bigness and value; to wit, a *Saphir* as broad as a twenty shillings piece, and half an inch thick; a *Ruby* full as great, but far richer; an E-

I *merauld*

merauld not inferiour to the rest ; a *Pearl* as big as an ordinary Walnut; a world of Diamonds and other lesser Stones, but all of so great value, that this *Cabinet*, with that which is in it, is valued to be worth five hundred thousand Crowns. Lastly, I saw here the great round Table made of Inlaid precious stones polished neatly ; A Table would make the most hungry Stomach forget its grumbling, whilst the eyes are fed upon the unroasted Birds, which together with curious flowers compose this admirable piece ; *Pearls, Rubies, Sapphires, Cornelian, Emeralds, Lapis Lazuli* &c. are employed here artificially to the making of these Birds and Flowers. You'll conceive better of this Table, when I shall tell you, that it's worth a hundred thousand Crowns, and that it was fifteen years in making, and yet thirty Men wrought at it daily. In the midst of it is the great Ball of the Arms of the Duke of *Florence* in precious stones.

The 5th. Cabinet.

The 5th. Cabinet standing at the further end of this Gallery, containeth the Altar and Tabernacle, which are to be set up in the new Chapel of S. *Laurence* described above. The Crystal Pillars curiously wrought, and being a full Ell long, with their *Capitelli* of pure Gold; the four like Pictures of precious Stones which were five years each of them in cutting : the Variety of other precious stones set thick here and there, and of great size: the neat contexture of other polished Stones of several colours and lustre : the pictures of inlaid precious stones, which compose the *Antependium* of the Altar : the variety of rich *Cameos* which

are

Part I. A **Voyage** to ITALY

are set here and there, and cut into Pictures: In fine, the whole composure of this Altar and Tabernacle, being the height of Wit and Riches, I can neither describe enough, nor you admire sufficiently.

4. Having thus seen the *Gallery* and adjoyning *Cabinets*, I was presently led into another quarter of this Palace, where I saw the Great Duke's *Argentaria*, or *Plate*. Entring into this great square Room I saw *twelve great Cupboards*, as high as the Room, set with excellent Plate in all kinds. In one of them they shewed me a whole service of beaten Gold, as Dishes, Plates, Forks, Spoons, Knives, with a world of other rich Vessels set in Gold ; also little Pictures in *miniature*; curious little Cabinets beset with Gold and Jewels; a *Turkish Scimetar* whose Handle and Scabbard of Gold, are thick set with Diamonds and precious Stones ; two other Swords with their Hilts of Gold curiously wrought with Diamonds ; a Dagger suitable to one of them, and of the same richness; a great Cross set thick with Diamonds, and other precious Stones, a rare Cup of one great *Emerauld*, with a cover to it of the same ; a Bason and Ewre of Gold set very thick with *Turky* Stones. In another Cupboard I saw great variety of Silver Plate in all kinds. In another they shewed me a Saddle and Bridle with Stirrups of Gold, all set thick with *Turky* Stones, Diamonds, Pearls, and other rich Stones, with the Saddle Cloth, or *Housse*, all embroidered with Gold and Pearl: this was a Present from the Emperor to the Grand Duke. In another Cupboard they shew-

The Argentaria.

ed me the four great Silver Bed-posts enamel'd here and there, and set with polished Stones of divers Colours: They were made for the Marriage Bed of the Great Princess, Daughter to the late Duke of *Orleans*. In another they shewed me a curious *Antependium* for for an Altar, all of beaten Gold set with Pearl, precious Stones, and the Picture of *Cosmus* the Second in the middle of it, of curious enammel'd work, with his Ducal Crown set with Diamonds very richly: all along this *Antependi*r. above runs an Inscription. in Letters composed of many Rubies each Letter being two fingers long, and importing these words:

COSMUS II. DEI GRATIA MAGNUS DUX ETRURIÆ EX VOTO.

In another Cupboard I was shown the Foot of an *Elan*, and a *Visard* all set, and covered with *Turky* Stones.

The great Hall.
5. Descending from hence, we were led into the great Hall of this Palace, a vast Room, painted on all sides of the Walls with bold Painting, representing the Victories of the *Florentines* antiently. Here it is that on *Midsummer-day* the Country People come and Dance before the Great Duke, and the best Dancers are recompensed with an Honourable reward.

The long Corridor.
6. From hence I was let into the long *Corridor*, or close Gallery, which runs from the New Palace to the Old, over the River, and over the tops of Houses, for the space of half a mile, with many Turnings and Windings. It'
ver

very usefull for the Prince when he will go see his precious Treasure in the old Palace, or else go privately and hear how Justice is ministred there. For the Great Duke *Francis* gave order to *Buontalenti*, a rare Architect, to break a Window from this *Corridor* into the great Room in the old Palace, where the Magistrates render Justice, but yet so privately, that none should perceive it. The Architect did it, by setting up there the Dukes Arms at large, and breaking a Window behind them so imperceptibly, that the Great Duke thro' the little Holes made in the six Boule's of his Arms, could both hear and see how Justice was rendred there by his Officers. And one day hearing a poor Woman oppressed by an unjust Sentence, he sent for the Judges, and reprehending them severely, he reversed the former Sentence, and hearing the Cause a-new himself, pronounced Sentence for the poor Woman.

7. This long *Corridor* led us to the new Palace, called the *Palazzo di Piti*, because it was begun to be built by *Luca Piti*, after the design of *Brunelleschi*: but the expences growing too great for *Piti*'s Purse, it was bought by the Mother of great *Cosmus* the II. and afterwards carried on by her to that perfection we now see it in; and which makes it one of the prime Palaces of *Europe*. The design of it (for it is not yet all quite built) is to be a perfect Roman H, with double Rooms on all sides. As you ascend up to it, by an easie ascent from the street, it presents you with a fair Broad-side of building, in which I counted two and twenty great Windows all in a row, and all alike, and all of them

The new Palace.

checkt

cheekt up on either side by fine Stone Pillars. The fashion of building in this Palace, as in most of the best Palaces of *Florence*, is that which they call in Architecture, *la maniera rustica*; where great Free-stones are made advancing a little one over the other. Entering into the Palace, we saw the fair Court; and in the end of it, the *Grotta* or Fountain with a large Bason, in which they keep Fish for present use. This Court is square, and open only on one side towards the Garden, but hedged in with a high Terrass of Stone, whose top is level with the ground of the Garden. Beyond this Terrass and Court, lies a fine green spot of ground level with the first Story of the Palace, and half compassed about with a demicircle of Laurel Trees high and thick. Under these Trees of the demicircle, rise up stone seats, six rows high, like the seats in an *Amphitheater*, and capable of two thousand Men, who may all sit here with ease, and behold the Sports of Cavalry which are often exhibited upon this fair green spot of ground by the Nobility: the Great Duke and the Court beholding all this from the Windows of the Palace, while the rest of the Nobility and Ladies are seated conveniently in the *Amphitheater* under the Trees. The rest of this Garden is curiously set forth with Thickets of Bays, close shady Walks, fine high open Walks over-looking both the Town and Country, great Ponds of Water, a world of Statues of Marble and Stone, a rare round Bason of Water, with Fountains, and much wetting sports; the place for Birds and Beasts, the curious Ice-House, and cool Cellar under it, where the melting

The Garden.

melting Ice dropping down upon the Barrels of Wine, refresh it so exceedingly, that in all my Life time I never drunk so cool as I did at the Tap in this Cellar. But to return again to the Palace from whence this Garden hath led me; from the Garden we ascended into the Chambers of the *Great Dukes* Apartment, *The Duke's* and found them most sumptuous, both for con- *Apart-* trivance and furniture. Some of them are *ment.* painted over head by *Pietro di Cortona* the prime Painter now living: others expect his return again from *Rome*, and scorn to be painted by any hand but his: In another Chamber we were shown the History of *Seleucus*, giving to his only Son *Antiochus* (languishing and pining away with the love of his Mother-in-Law) his own beloved Wife *Stratonica*; shewing by this strange and unick example, that Paternal Love is greater than Conjugal. All this is rarely painted upon the Wall over the Hangings. In annother Chamber (the *Great Dukes* Chamber of Audience) I saw a Suit of Hangings valued at a hundred and fifty thousand Crowns: The *Arare Suit* Ground of them is Cloth of Gold upon which *of Hang-* are embroidered a world of Birds, Beasts, *ings.* Flowers, Trees, Rivers, Landskips in Silk and Silver; and in such a rich manner, that I take this to be one of the fairest Suits of Hangings in *Europe*: In another Chamber here I saw a rare Collection of Pictures, all Originals, and of the best hands in the world, *Titian's*, *Raphael's*, *Michael Angelo's*, *Andrea del Sarto's*, and many others. The best of them is that of *Raphael*, and painted by his own hand. This is the best Collection of Pictures that I ever saw, and

I 4   it

it belongs to Prince *Leopold* the Great Dukes Brother and a great *Virtuoso*. In the Great Dutchesses Chamber I saw half a dozen of excellent pieces of *Raphael* and others. In another Chamber (the Dukes Bed-chamber) we saw his curious *Therometers*, or Weather-Glasses; which are most curious. In another Chamber (the Doors being set open for the nonce) we looked through sixteen Chambers at once, and all of them fair great Rooms upon one Floor. And after all the Rooms of this House (as, the Cool, low Summer Room, the Masking Room, the several Apartments of the Great Prince Son of the Great Duke, and of Cardinal *John Carlo*, *Prince Matthias*, and *Prince Leopold*, all three Brothers of the *Great Duke*, and all lodging at once in this great Palace) by special favour we got the sight of the *Great Dukes fair Diamond*, which he always keeps under Lock and Key. It's absolutely the fairest in *Europe*, it weigheth 138 *Carats*, and it's almost an inch thick: and then our Jewellers will tell you what it's worth. I am sure *Monsieur Simonet* in *Lyons* (a famous Jeweller) to whom I shewed the weight and thickness of it, valued it to be richly worth a hundred thousand Crowns between Merchant and Merchant; and a hundred and fifty thousand Crowns between Prince and Prince.

The famous Diamond.

8. Going from the Great Dukes Palace, we fell presently upon the *Augustins Church*. This is a neat Church designed by *Brunellefchi*, and much beautified with handsome Pillars. The Tabernacle and high Altar cost a hundred thousand Crowns, and yields to few in *Italy* for neatness and state. Behind the High Altar in the

The Augustins Church.

Part I. *A Voyage to* ITALY.

the very end of the Church, is a rare Picture of our *Saviour* absolving the poor Woman catched in Adultery. The confusion that appears in the Face of this Woman, makes it appear what a rare Painter *Allori* was, who made this Picture.

9. Passing from hence over the Bridge (where four white Marble Statues representing the four seasons of the year, stand, all made by *Michael Angelo*) we came to the *Piazza* of the *Gran Duca*, where I saw the *Equestrian Statue* of *Cosmus* the Great in *Bronze*, with his Victories and prime actions in the Pedestal of the same Metal. At the corner of the old Palace in this *Piazza*, stands the brave Fountain, with a *Neptune*, *Tritons*, and *Nereides*. Near the Gates of the Palace here, stand two Statues of more than Gygantean bulk: that of *David* is the hand of *Michael Angelo*: and that of *Hercules* killing *Cacus* is of the hand of *Bandinelli*. The other Statues here in the *Portico* hard by, are much cry'd up for rare Pieces, as that of *Perseus* in Brass; that of the rape of the *Sabins* in Marble; and that of *Judith* in Brass, holding a Sword in one hand, and *Holofernes* his head in the other.

The Piazza.

10. Looking up from this *Piazza* to the top of the Palace, I beheld the high *Tower* mounted thereupon. It's a hundred and fifty yards from the ground, and which is the wonder, it hath no other foundation than the Wall of the Palace and the top of the House: Hence it's said that the *Florentines* have three wonderful Towers: one in the Air, to wit, this Tower: another in the Water, to wit, the *Fanal* of *Legorne*:

Three admirable Towers.

and

and the third in the Earth, to wit, the *Campanile* of *Florence*, whose Foundations are exceeding deep in the ground.

11. Going from the *Piazza* towards the *Domo*, we were presently stopt by the Church of S. *Michael*, a square flat Church, whose outside is adorned with rare Statues. The best are, that of S. *Matthew* in brass made by *Laurentius Cion* : that of S. *Thomas* in brass touching the side of our Saviour, with great demonstration of diffidence in his looks, is of *Andrea Parrochios* hand. That of S. *Peter* in Marble is excellent for the *Drapery* of it. That of S. *George* in Marble is compared to the best in *Rome*, and hath been praised both in *Prose* and *Verse*: that of St. *Mark* hath so grave and honest a Countenance, that *Michael Angelo* (a competent Judge) stopping one day to behold it, and being asked what he thought of it, answered, if St. *Mark* had such a countenance as this, as it's likely he had, a Man might almost, for his looks sake, believe all that he wrote.

The Church of Saint Michael.

12. Going from hence we were presently at the *Domo*. This, I believe, was the finest Church in *Italy* when it was built. It was anciently called S. *Reparata* Church; but since it is called *Santa Maria Florida*, a fit name for the Cathedral of *Florence*. The Foundations and Architecture of it were contrived by *Arrolfo di Lapo*, a *Dutchman*, and *a la maniera rustica*, saith *Vasari* of it, in his Lives of Painters. It's one of the neatest Churches without that I ever beheld; being clad in white, red, and black Marble, but it's only white plastered within, with

The Domo.

Pillars

Part I. A Voyage to ITALY.

Pillars of a dark coloured Free-stone. It seems as if the Architect of this Church had been somewhat of *Diogenes* his mind: and as the latter thought the World would be turned up-side down one day; so the former might be of opinion that the World would be turned inside out, and that then this Church would be the fairest in the World, and all lined with Marble: As it is, it looks a little Hypocritically; tho' the Structure within be of a notable contrivance. On the top of it stands mounted a fair *Cupola*, (or *Tholus*) made by *Brunellefchi* a *Florentine*. This was the first *Cupola* in *Europe*; and therefore the more admirable for having no Idea after which it was framed; and for being the Original even of that of S. *Peters* in *Rome*, after which so many young *Cupola*'s in *Rome*, and elsewhere, have been made since. Hence it is said, that *Michael Angelo* coming now and then to *Florence* (his Native Country) whiles he was making the *Cupola* in *Rome* of S. *Peters* Church, and viewing attentively this *Cupola* of *Florence*, used to say to it; *Come, se non voglio, meglio di te non poffo.* It's said also, that *Brunellefchi* making this *Cupola*, caused Taverns, Cook-shops and Lodgings to be set in it, that the Workmen might find all things necessary there, and not spend time in going up and down: and he had reason, for this *Cupola* from the ground below, to the top of all the *Lantern*, is *two hundred and two Braccie* or yards high. The straight Passage from the top of the *Cupola* to the round Brazen Ball, is thirty six yards high. The Ball is four yards wide, and capable of four and twenty Men: and the Cross at the top of this Ball eight yards

The Cupola

yards long, The ſtraight Paſſage upon the Ball is neatly contrived like a round Chimney of white Marble, with holes on both ſides, and brazen ſteps croſs thoſe holes to climb up eaſily by hand and foot, the paſſage being clean and ſmooth. From the top of this *Cupola*, taking a perfect view of *Florence* under us, and of the whole Country about it, with the ſight of two thouſand Villa's or Country Houſes, ſcattered here and there, round about the Town, we came down again to view the inſide of this Church. It is about three hundred Foot long, from the great Door to the Quire, and from thence to the end almoſt two hundred more. The Quire is round and perpendicularly under the *Cupola*, being of the ſame bigneſs; and, upon ſolemn days, when the wax Candles are lighted round about it, it looks gloriouſly: otherwiſe in winter time it ſeems too dark. The High Altar, which ſtands in this Quire, is plain like thoſe of ancient Cathedrals, and adorned with a rare Statue of a dead Jeſus in white Marble, made by the hand of *Bandinelli*. Looking up from the Quire to the Cupola, you ſee it painted on the inſide with a repreſentation of Heaven, Hell and Purgatory; The Painters were *Georgio Vaſari*, and *Thaddeo Zucchari*. Behind the Higher Altar are the rare Statues of *Adam* and *Eve*, by the hand of *Bandinelli*. Near the Door of the Sacriſty you may read an inſcription, importing how that in this Town of *Florence* had been held a General Council, where the Re-union of the *Latin* and *Greek Church* had been made. The Golden *Diploma* of this union written both in *Latin* and *Greek*, and ſubſcrib'd

unto

unto by the hands of the Pope and Cardinals on the one side; and by the Emperor of *Constantinople*, with the Patriarch of *Constantinople*, and the *Greek* Bishops on the other side; to which are put the Leaden Seal of the Pope, and the Golden Seal of the said Emperor; It is kept in the Archives, or Registers of *Bologna*. In this Council both the Pope of *Rome*, *Eugenius* IV. and *Palæologus* the Emperour of *Constantinople*, were present, with the Cream of Bishops, both of the Eastern and Western Churches; and in this Council not only the Procession of the Holy Ghost from the Father and the Son was favourably vindicated; but also that there was an Essay that Purgatory should be proved to the *Greeks*, out of their own Fathers as well as from the *Latins*; and divers other points of Ceremony and Practice were asserted and great endeavours made that they should be established. Unto all which it is pretended that the said Emperor and Patriarch, and the other *Greek* Bishops (except only *Marcus Ephesinus*) subscribed; as did also the *Armenians*, *Ethiopians*, *Georgians*, and *Jacobites*, who all hereupon were admitted to Communion by the Roman Church. In fine, in this Church you see the Statues of divers Saints, who have been Archbishops of this Town; and the Tombs of divers Famous Men; as of *Marsilius Ficinus* the Platonick Christian Philosopher; of *Dante* the *Florentine Poet*, whose true Picture is yet to be seen here in a red Gown: of *Joannes Acutius* an *English* Knight, and sometimes General of the *Pisani*, as the old Gothick Letters set high upon the Wall under his Picture on Horseback, told me. Yet

Leandro Alberti Descript. Ital.

The Council of Florence.

Ver-

Verstegan will not have him to have been called Sir *John Sharp*, but Sir *John Hackwood*. But it imports little to me what his name was, seeing he was a brave *Englishman*, and deserved to have his Tomb and Inscription here, and his Picture among the other Worthies in the *Dukes Gallery*. Here's also in this Church the Tomb of *Brunellefchi*, or *Philippus Brunaltins*, who made the *Cupola* of this Church; as also the Tomb of *Giotto*, who made the *Campanile*, or fine Steeple here. And in fine, here lies *Cimabue* the famous Painter of his time. It was he that first restored Painting again, which had been lost for many year in *Italy*, and taught it to *Giotto*, *Gaddi*, *Taffi*, and others, who carried it on to a great height.

In his restitution of decayed Intelligence.

See Baker in Edward the Third.

Vassari in the Lives of Painters, in Cimabue.

The Campanile.

13. Near to the *Domo* stands the *Campanile*, or *high Steeple of Florence* made by *Giotto*. It's a hundred and fifty *Braccie*, or little yards high, and half as deep in the ground. It's flat at top and crusted all over with curious little polished Marble Stones, Marble Pillars, and Statues; so that, (as *Charles* the V. said of it) if it had a case to cover it withal, and hinder it from being seen too frequently, Men would flock thither at the taking off of this cover, as to see a wonder. Indeed it's a kind of wonder, to see that in three hundred years space, not the least part of that Steeple (all crusted over with Marble) is perished. There are divers good Statues on all sides of it, but the best of them all is that of the *Zuccone*, or *Bald Man*, made by *Donatello*, which he himself esteemed so much, that when he would affirm any thing seriously, he used to say, *Alla fe ch'io porto al mio Zuccone*: and the fame

fame *Donatello* having finished it, spoke to it, in Jest, and said; *Favella, borfu, favella; o ti venga il cacafangue*; such good conceits have fantastical Men of themselves and their own works.

14. Near to the *Domo* also, stands the *Baptistery*, or round Church of St. *John*, where all the Children of the Town are Baptized. The Brazen Doors of it (three in all) are admirable, especially that which looks towards the Great Church, of which *Michael Angelo* being asked his opinion, answer'd, That it was so well made, that it might stand at the entrance of Paradise. These Doors are all of Brass historied into figures, containing the Remarkable Histories of both the Testaments. They were the work of brave *Laurentius Cion*, who spent fifty years in making them: a long time, I confess; but, this is it which *Appelies* called *æternitati pingere*, to work things that will out-last Brass, and be famous for ever. Within this *Baptistery* I saw a Statue of St. *Mary Magdalen* of the hand of *Donatello*; and it's a rare piece, if you consider *Magdalen* in her Pennance. Here's also a neat Tomb of *Baltassar Cossa*, once called *John* the XXIV, but deposed in the Council of *Constance* for the Peace of the Church. The Tomb of this *Baltassar* looking somewhat like a Cradle, may be called the Cradle of the greatness of the *Medicean* Family. For some Writers say, that *Cosmus Medices*, firnam'd afterwards *Pater Patria*, being Heir of this *Baltassar Cossa* (who died at *Florence*, in the House of *John Medices*) with the Money that he found belonging to him after his death, did such good Deeds to the peo-

The Baptisterio.

Alfonso Loschi in his Compend. Histo.

ple

ple, that he won to himself the name of *Pater Patriæ*; and to his Family that credit which got it afterwards the supream command.

15. I cannot omit here to take notice of a little round *Pillar* in the *Piazza*, near this Baptistery, with the figure of a Tree in iron nail'd to it, and old words engraven upon it, importing, that in this very place stood anciently an Elm-Tree, which being touched casually by the Hearse of St. *Zenobius*, as they carried it here in Procession, the Tree presently hereupon budded forth with green Leaves of sweet Odour, though in the Month of *January*. In memory of which Miracle, this Pillar was set up in the same place for a memorial.

The Church of S.Mark. 16. From thence going to the Church of St *Mark* belonging to the *Dominicans*, I saw there the Tomb of S. *Antoninus*, Archbishop once of this Town, and Friar of this order. The Tomb is under the Altar, in a neat Chapel on the left hand, made by *John di Bologna*. In this Church also I saw a rare Picture of S. *Mark*, made by *Bartholomeo del Frate*, it stands full in your sight as you enter into the Church; and a Man must be blind not to see it, and dull not to like it. On the left hand, as you enter into the Church, is the Tomb of *Picus Mirandula*, commonly called the Phœnix of Princes, with this Epitaph written upon the side of the Wall;

*Joannes jacet hic Mirandula, cætera norunt.
Et Tagus & Ganges, forsan & Antipodes.*

Near

Near this Tomb is a fine Picture upon an Altar, where two little Angels are made playing upon Musical Instruments. These Angels are held to be the rarest Pieces that can be seen in Painting. They are of the hand of *Bartholomeo del Frate*. In the Convent of these Friars I saw often their Still-House, where they make and sell excellent Extractions and Cordial Waters. There is also a neat Library here filled with good Books.

17. Turning from hence on the left hand, I came presently to the *Annunciata*, a place of great Devotion. The Pictures of Faith and Charity over the Arch in the *Antiporto*, or open Porch built upon Pillars, are of the hand of *Jacomo Pontorno*, being but yet nineteen years old; which, when *Michael Angelo* first saw, he said, This *Jacomo*, if he continue thus, will carry up Painting to the skies. Entering into the little Court that stands before the *Church Door*, you see it painted round about in *Fresco* by rare hands. Those Pieces that *Andrea del Sarto* made, are the best, and his Head in white Marble is set in the Wall. In the Cloister, over the door that goes into the Church, is seen a rare Picture in *Fresco*, upon the Wall of the hand of *Andrea del Sarto*. It represents the Virgin Mother with our Saviour upon her knee, and St. *Joseph* in a cumbent posture, leaning upon a Sack full stuft, and reading in a Book. The Picture is admirable for sweetness and majesty, and is called *La Madonna del Sacco*, and it got *Andrea* such credit, that *Titian* himself preferred it before all the pieces he had ever seen, and used often to say, that it grieved him, that he could not

The Annunciata.

often satiate his sight with the beholding of so rare a Picture; and *Michael Angelo* talking once in *Rome* with *Raphael Urbin* concerning Painters, said thus to him: There is *vn huom corso*, a little fellow in *Florence* (meaning this *Andrea*) who had he been employed in great matters as thou art, would make thee sweat again. *Virtuosi* make a great dispute which of those three Painters was the most excellent: *Raphael Urbin*, *Michael Angelo* or *Andrea del Sarto*. But the wisest give every one his particular praise, or excelliency: *Raphael* was excellent in *colori*: *Michael Angelo* in *design*: and *Andrea* in making things seem to be of *relievo*, and look as God made them, that is, pulpy, and rising up like living flesh. Having thus admired the work of *Andrea*, we entred into the Church of the *Annunciata*, and there saw the curious Silver Altar, behind which, upon the Wall, is kept the miraculous Picture of the *Annunciation*, which gives the name of *Annunciata* to this Church. The little Picture of our Saviour, about a foot and half long, which is seen upon the out-side of the Tabernacle, is of the foresaid *Andrea's* hand, and much esteemed. In this Church lieth buried *Baccio Bandinelli*, a famous Sculptor, in a curious Marble Tomb, with his own and his Wives Pictures engraven in Marble with his own hand. Behind the Quire lies buried *Joannes di Bo'gna*, a famous Sculptor also, as his several works in *Florence* shew him to have been; as the *Rape* of the *Sabins* before the old Palace. The *Centaure* in the Streets. The Chapel of S. *Antoninus* in S. *Marks* Church. This Chapel in the *Annunciata* here, and the golden Horse and Man

Man spoken of above in the Duke's Armory, do witness.

18. From hence, having first seen the *Statue* of the Great Duke. *Ferdinand* on Horseback in Brass, which stands in the *Piazza* before the *Annunciata*, I went to the Church of the *Francescans*, called *Santo Croce*. This Church is of a large bulk and height, but somewhat too dark. The side Altars are many, and cheeked with round Pillars, and adorned with excellent Pictures. The *Pulpit* would become a *Chryfoftome*, or a *Chryfologue*: It's of white Marble, in which are graven the most notable Actions of S. *Francis* in *a baffo relievo*. I never beheld it, but I found some new graces in it. Somewhat behind it, near to a little door, is the Tomb of *Michael Angelo*, the *Trifmegift* of *Italy*, being the greatest *Painter*, the greatest *Sculptor*; the greatest Architect of his time. Hence over his Tomb, and under his Picture, are placed three Women in white Marble representing Architecture, Painting and Sculpture, holding in their hands the several Instruments belonging to these professions. If you ask me whither of the two, Painting, or Sculpture; is to be preferred, though a blind Man being chosen judge once of this question, when he was given to understand that in the smooth Painting there were Heads, Arms, Legs, Hands and Feet, as well as in the bulky Statue which he had felt, judged presently for Painting ; yet *Michael Angelo* himself preferred Sculpture before Painting as the Body is to be preferred before the Superficies of a Body. But to return again to the Tomb of this great Artist, I found some words

S. and r. Croces.

upon the Tombstone, but those so dull and hard to be read in that dark corner, that one in the Company chose rather to make him a new Epitaph, than read that which is written there: and it was this;

Cur indignemur mortales morte perire?
Ecce, stupor mundi! hic Angelus ipse perit.

And I think the modern *Roman* was of the same mind too, when he chose also to make him this Epitaph:

Roma mihi mortem tribuit, Florentia vitam:
Nemo aliis vellet nasci, & obire, locis.

In the midst of this Church I found buried an *English* Bishop, called *Catrick*, who had been Embassador here from *England*, and likely in the time of the Council of *Florence*. His Arms were three Cats Argent in a Sable Field. In fine, at the very end of this *Church*, on the left hand stands a neat Chapel, with a painted Cupola, belonging to the Family of the *Nicolini*, in which Chapel there are excellent Statues and Pictures.

The Abbey. 19. Not far from hence stands the *Abbadia*, an Abbey of *Benedictin Monks*. In the Church is the Tomb of the Founder of this Abbey, a *German* Nobleman, call'd *Comte Hugo*, who commanded *Toscany* under the Emperor *Otho* the III. The occasion of building this Monastery and many others by this *Hugo*, is too long to tell, and perchance would not find belief every where. It's told publickly every year upon

S. Tho-

Part I. *A Voyage to* ITALY.

S. *Thomas* his day in high Mass time here, by some one or other of the chief Wits of the *Academy* of the *Crusca*: But I must beg pardon of the curious, if I desire them to go and hear it there, as I did.

20. From thence I went to the Church of *Santa Maria Novella* belonging to the *Dominicans*. Here it is, that the Council of *Florence* spoken of above, was held. There are many good Pictures in this Church, as also divers neat Tombs of holy Men and Women, and others: among which, that of *Joseph*, Patriarch of *Constantinople*. *S. Maria Novella.*

21. Returning from hence along the River side, we came to the High Pillar with the Statue of Justice in *Porphyry* upon it. It was erected here, because it was in this very place where *Cosmus* the Great heard the news of the reduction of *Siena*. A witty Nobleman seeing this Statue of Justice upon so high a Pillar, said, that Justice here was too high placed for poor Men to arrive to it. Another observ'd, that Justice there turns her back to the Courts of Justice, which stand not far from thence. *The Statue of Justice.*

22. Having seen the chief things in the Town, I visited some places out of the Town; and chiefly, the *Poggio Imperiale*, a Villa, belonging to the Great Dutchess, and about a good mile distant from the Town. In this house I saw rare Pictures, and great store of them, the House being furnished with nothing else. In one Gallery are the true Pictures of divers late Princes of the House of *Austria*, of the House of *Medices*, and of other Princes their Allies. In other Rooms we saw a world of rare Pictures *Poggio Imperiale.*

K 3   as

as the *Venus* of *Titian*, though I think it be but a Copy: the admirable S. *Hierom* of *Alberto Durero*: a *Magdalen* of *Raphael's* hand: a St. *John Baptist* of *Caravagio's* hand: an *Adam* and *Eve* of *Alberto Durero*: A Piece of *Pietro Perugino's*, Virgin Mother with our Saviour dead upon her knee: S. *John Evangelist*, and three other Persons standing, or kneeling by, with weeping Faces, and most sad looks; it's one of the most moving Pieces that I ever beheld. Then the Picture of the Assumption of our Lady in the Chapel, of the hand of *Andrea del Sarto*; with a World of other most exquisite Pictures. The little neat Oratory in this House, called the Oratory of the *Great Dutchess*, curiously inlaid into Flowers, by polished Stones of divers colours; that is, a whole closet of shining Marble inlaid into Flowers, is the neatest little Room that ever I saw. In fine, the little *Grotto*, and the Statue of *Adonis* made by the hand of *Michael Angelo* are much esteemed.

Pratolino. 23. Another day we went to *Pratolino*, a Villa of the Great Duke, some six miles distant from *Florence*. Here we saw in the Garden excellent Grots, Fountains, Water-works, Shady-Walks, Groves, and the like, all upon the side of a Hill. Here you have the *Grotto* of *Cupid* with the wetting-stools, upon which, sitting down, a great Spout of Water comes full in your Face. The *Fountain of the Tritons* overtakes you so too, and washeth you soundly. Then being led about this Garden, where there are store of Fountains under the Laurel Trees, we were carried back to the *Grots* that are under

der the ſteirs, and ſaw there the ſeveral *Guiochi d' Aqua*: as that of *Pan* ſtriking up a melodious tune upon his Mouth-Organ at the ſight of his *Miſtriſi*, appearing over againſt him: that where the *Angel* carries a Trumpet to his Mouth, and ſoundeth it; and where the *Country Clown* offers a Diſh of Water to a *Serpent*, who drinks of it, and lifteh up his head when he hath drunk: that of the *Mill* which ſeems to break and grind Olives: the *Paper Mill*: the *Man* with the *Grinding-Stone*: the *Sarazens* head gaping and ſpewing out Water: the *Grotto* of *Galatea*, who comes out of a Door in a *Sea Chariot* with two *Nymphs*, and ſaileth a while upon the Water, and ſo returns again in at the ſame Door: the curious round *Table* capable of twelve or fifteen Men, with a curious *Fountain* playing conſtantly in the midſt of it, and places between every Treacher or Perſon, for every Man to ſet his bottle of Wine in cold Water: the *Samaritan Woman* coming out of her Houſe with her Buckets to fetch Water at the Fountain, and having filled her Buckets, returns back again the ſame way: in the mean time you ſee Smiths thumping, Birds chirping in Trees, Mills grinding, and all this is done by water, which ſets theſe little inventions a-work, and makes them move as it were of themſelves: in the mean time an Organ plays to you, while you dine there in *Freſco* at that Table, if you have meat. Then the neat Bathing Place, the Pillar of petrefied Water, and laſtly, the great Pond and *Grotta* before the Houſe, with the huge *Gyant* ſtooping to catch at a *Rock* to throw it at *Heaven*. This Gyant is ſo big, that within the very Tigh of

K 4   him

136 A Voyage to ITALY. Part I.

him is a great *Grotto* of Water, called the *Grotto* of *Thetis*, and the Shell-Fishes all spouting out Water.

Lampeggio. 24. I went also to *Lampeggio*, a Villa some five miles distant from *Florence*, belonging to Prince *Matthias*. It's curiously adorned with Pictures, especially Battles of the hand of *Tempesta*. Here I saw a curious Cabinet of Coral and enamell'd work. The fine *Giuoco di Mecha* or *Turkish play*, the curious Glasses, and little Armory.

The Stables. 25. Returning to the Town again, we saw the Great Duke's Stables full of excellent well managed Horses.

The Wild Beasts. 26. Near to the Stables stands the Seraglio where the Wild Beasts are kept, which are often made to fight one with another. Here I saw Lyons, Leopards, Tygers, Bears, Wolves, Wild Boars and Foxes, all which they can let out severally at the Doors of their several Dens, into a fair Court to fight, and when they have done, they can bring them back again into their Dens by a fearful *Machine* of wood made like a great *Green Dragon*, which a Man within it rouls upon wheeles; and holding out two lighted Torches at the Eyes of it, frights the fiercest Beast thereby into his Den. The Prince and the Court in the mean time standing high above may see the Combats of these wild Beasts with ease and without danger. I have read,

In the Chronology that a *Lyon* here once escaping out of this place *of* by chance, and running up and down the *Romual-* Streets, met at last (all others flying into houses) *dus to. 1.* a little Child, who had neither fear nor wit *pag. 15.* enough to ... retire: and seized upon him. The Mo-

Mother of the Child hearing in what cafe he was, ran out prefently, and cafting her felf upon her knees with Tears in her eyes, and humble poftures of Supplication, moved fo the *Lyon* to pity, that he rendered her the Child without hurting it, or her.

27. I faw alfo here divers Palaces of Noblemen upon occafion of their Feftine. For it is the Cuftom here in Winter to invite the Chief Ladies of the Town (Married Women only) to come to play at Cards in Winter Evenings for three or four hours fpace ; and this one night in one Palace, another night in another Palace. Thither the Ladies go, and find the Houfe open to all Comers and Goers both Ladies and Gentlemen, that are of any Garb. In every Chamber the doors are fet open, and for the moft part you fhall fee eight or ten Chambers on a floor, going out of one another, with a fquare Table holding eight Perfons, as many Chairs, two Silver Candlefticks with Wax lights in them, and ftore of lights round about the Room. At the hour appointed, Company being come, they fit down to play, a Cavalier fitting between every Lady, and all the Women as fine in Clothes and Jewels, as if they were going to a Ball. The Doors of all thefe Rooms being open, the light great, the Women glittering, and all glorious, you would take thefe Palaces to be the Enchanted Palaces of the old King of the Mountains. Any Gentlemen may come into thefe Palaces and ftand behind the Gamefters, and fee both how modeftly they play, and how little they play for. In the mean time there's a Side-Chamber always open

for Gentlemen to into, and refresh themselves with Wine standing in Snow, or with Limonade, or some such cooling Drinks, which are also offered to the Ladies. In a great Room below, at the entrance of the Palace, there is a long Table for Gamesters that love to play deep, that is, that love to play only for Money,

Their Sports.

The *Florentines* enjoying by the goodness and Wisdom of their excellent Prince, the fruits of Peace, have many other Recreations, where the People pass their time chearfully, and think not of Rebellion by muttering in corners. For this reason, both in Winter and Summer they have their several Divertisements. In Winter their *Giuoco di Calcio* (a play something like our Foot-ball, but that they play with their hands) every night from the Epiphany till Lent, with their *Principi di Calcio*. This being a thing particular to *Florence*, deserves to be described. The two Factions of the *Calcio*, the Red and the Green, choose each of them a Prince, some young Cavalier of a good Purse. These Princes being chosen, choose a world of Officers, and lodge, for the time, in some great Palace; where they keep their *Courts*, receive Embassadors, from one another, and give them publick Audience in State, send Post to one another complain of one anothers Subjects, and take Prisoners from one another; hear their Councellors one after another, disswading from, or perswading to War; give Orders for settling their Affairs at home, hear the Complaints of their Subjects, jeer their Enemy Princes in Embassies, and at last resolve to fight, with proclaiming

Il Giuoco di Calcio.

claiming War. During thefe ferious Treaties, which laft for many nights, the Secretaries of State (two prime wits) read before their feveral *Princes Bills* for regulating and reforming the abufes of their Subjects; and read openly Petitions and Secret Advices: in all which they jeer a world of people in the Town, and fhow prodigious Wit. In fine, having fpun out thus the time till near *Carnavale* or *Shrove-tide*, the two Princes refolve on a Battle at *Calcio*, to be fought in the Piazza of *Santa Croce*, before the Great Duke and Court. Upon the day appointed, the two Princes of the *Calcio* come to the place in a moft ftately *Cavalcata*, with all the young Noblemen and Gentlemen of the Town, upon the beft Horfes they can find, with Scarffs red or green, about their Arms. Having made their feveral *Cavalcataes* before the Great Dukes Throne or Scaffold, they light from their Horfes and enter into the Lifts with Trumpets founding before them, and accompanied with a Stately Train, and with their Combatants in their feveral Liveries. Having ranked themfelves a pretty diftance one from the other, their Standard Bearers at found of Trumpet, carry both at once, their Standards to the foot of the *Great Dukes Scaffold*. This done, the Ball, or Ballon is thrown up in the midft between them, and to it they go with great nimblenefs, flight and difcretion; and fometimes they fall to it indeed, and cuff handfomely: but upon pain of Death, no Man muft refent, afterwards out of the Lifts, what ever happened here; but all animofities arifing here, end here too. At laft, that fide which

throws

throws or ſtrikes the *Ballan* over the Rails of the other ſide, wins the day, and runs to the Standards, which they carry away till night, at what time the Conquering Prince entertains them at a *Feſtino di Ballo* at Court, made to ſome Lady, and where all his Chief Officers and Combatants dance alone with the Ladies at the Ball, none elſe being permitted to dance with them that night. Beſides theſe Paſtimes, they have once a week, dancing at the Court, from Twelfth-day till Lent, at which Balls, all the Ladies of the Town are invited, to the number ſometimes of two hundred, and theſe all married Women, and all invited by a particular Ticket. Then the ſeveral Opera's or Muſical *Dramata* are acted and ſung with rare Coſt and Art. Laſtly, their publick running at the Ring, or at the *Fauchin*, for a piece of Plate. And in Summer, they have their ſeveral Dancing days, and their frequent *Corſi di Palio* upon certain known days, and for known *Prizes*, and all before the good Prince, who countenanceth all theſe Sports with his Preſence, thinking wiſely, that there's leſs hurt in publick Mirth, than in private Mutinies.

Other Paſtimes.

Having ſaid thus much of *Florence*, I will now ſay ſomething of the Court, the Government, Strength, Gentry, Riches, Intereſt, Language, and Learned Men of this Town.

The Court.

For the Court, it's clearly one of the beſt of *Italy*. Great Riches make it look plump, and give it an excellent *en bon point*. The Noble *Palace*, the Prince, his Title of *Sereniſſimo*, his Train and Retinue of Noble Officers and Gentlemen, his ſtore of *Pages*, *Palfreniers*, *Guards*

of

Part I. A Voyage to ITALY.

of *Swissers* with Halbards, his Troop of Horse, waiting upon him, make this *Court* appear splendid. The Duke himself also, who makes this Court, makes it a fine Court. His extraordinary Civility to Strangers, made us think our selves at home there. He was above Fifty, and hath an Austrian Look and Lip, which his Mother, *Magdalena* of *Austria*, Sister to the Emperor *Ferdinand* the II. lent him. He admits willingly of the visits of Strangers, if they be Men of condition; and he receives them in the midst of his Audience-Chamber standing; and will not discourse with them, till they be covered too. It's impossible to depart from him disgusted, because he pays your Visit with as much Wit as Civility: and having entertain'd you in his Chamber with Wise discourse, he will entertain you in your own Chamber too with a *Regalo* of dainty Meats and Wines, which he will be sure to send you. The *Great Dutchess* too is another main Pillar of this Court. She is of the House of the Duke of *Urbin*, once a Soveraign Prince in *Italy*, but now extinct in her Father, who was the last Duke: and she had been Soveraign of that Dutchy, had she been of the Soveraign Sex: but what Nature refused her in Sex, it hath given her in Beauty, and so made her a Greater Soveraign, ever of *Florence*. Of her the Great Duke hath two Sons. *Cosmus* the Prince of *Toscany* married one of the Daughters of the late Duke of *Orleans*. A great Traveller, and one that visited most of the Princes Courts of *Christendom*. The Name of this Family is *Medices*; a Family which hath given to the Church four Popes, and

The Great Duke.

The Great Dutchess.

to

The Medi-
cean Famil-
ly.

See Alfon-
so Lofchi
in his
compend.
Hiftor.

to *France* two Queens. This Family is ancient, and came firſt out of *Athens*. It was always confiderable during the Republick of *Florence*, but far more, ſince it hath got the ſtart of all the other Families ſo far, as to become their Sovereign. The beginning of the greatneſs of this Family came from *Coſmus Medices*, ſirnamed *Pater Patriæ*. This Man being very rich and of a liberal mind, ſpent four hundred thouſand Crowns in publick and private buildings, one hundred thouſand Crowns more in loan Moneys to the poor Citizens. Theſe Generous Actions, which ſhould have got him the love of all Men, purchaſed him the hatred of ſome of the great Ones, who accuſing him of affecting Soveraignty, raiſed a ſtrong Faction againſt him. The heads of this Faction were *Rinaldo Albizzi*, *Pala Strozzi*, *Ridolfo Peruzzi*, and *Nicolo Barbadori*. Theſe Men corrupting the Suffrages of the *Senate*, cauſed *Coſmus* to be clapt up, with an intention to take away his Life. *Coſmus* in Priſon fearing poyſon, abſtained from Meats four days together, and almoſt died of Hunger, for fear of being killed with poyſon: At laſt he was reſcued from this melancholy humor by his honeſt Keeper; who gave him ſuch aſſurances: that he ſhould not be poyſon'd that he took Meat again, and kept in his vital Breath, which was almoſt come to his lips. Then his Keeper (not content to be half courteous) having recover'd his Body, ſtrove to recover his Mind too, which was ſore ſpent with Fears and Melancholy; and for this purpoſe brought unto him the *Buffon* of *Bernardo Guadagni* then *Confanoliero*, the Chief Magiſtrate of the Republick,

Republick, who with his Witty Jests, so cheered him up with mirth, that he began not only to think of living again, but also of getting out from thence, that he might live long. To this end he works with the *Buffon* to carry a promise in Writing from him to the *Confaloniero*, of 1000 Crowns of Gold, upon condition he would free him. The *Buffon* undertakes it, and money takes with the *Confanoliero*, who under pretence of examining the Cause to put him to Death, finds him only worthy of Banishment, to which he condemns him; and the place of his Banishment was *Venice*. This was it that he desired, for being at *Venice*, he wrought so well by Friends with the People, that loved him, that he was restored again to his Cóuntry, and got the Title of *Pater Patriæ* by a publick decree. By this Title his Family grew into that esteem, that it overtopt the rest, and in time wrought it self into Soveraignty.

For the Government of *Florence*, it is now Monarchical and Despotical, the Great Dukes Will being absolute, all great businesses passing thro' his knowledge and liking: so that he wants nothing of a King, but the Name; and that too he almost hath under the Name of Great Duke. *The Government*.

As for the Strength of this State, it hath 20 Episcopal Cities; 500 little Walled Towns; strong Forts on the Confines: and can make an Army of Forty thousand Foot, three thousand Horse, twelve Gallies, two Galleasses, two Galleons, and twenty Ships of War. *The Strength*.

For

The Gentry of Florence.

For the Gentry, they are both Ingenious and Rich. The subtil Air of this Country, and the Academy of the *Crusca* have sharpned them into much Wit; and their good Husbandry, and under-hand Traffick hath put them notably into Purse. For they think it no disgrace to have a *Banco* at home, and meet daily at the Exchange about Traffick and Trading; while their Wives take their Pleasure in riding in a good Coach and attended by handsom Liveries. This makes them hold up their Nobility by the Chin, and not only preserves their Families from sinking, but rather makes them swim in a full Sea of Honour; for they are by this means enabled to buy Great Offices for their Children in other Courts, whereby they often make them mount to the Highest Dignities; when they are there, no Man reproaches unto them the way they took to come thither, whether by Water, or by Land; by Traffick, or by the Sword; by the School-Book, or Count-Book. If the *French* Gentry would follow this way, they might have Shooes and Stockings for their Children (which some of them want in the Country) wherewith to keep their Noble Blood warm in Winter.

Riches.

For the Riches of this Prince, they are about a *Million and a half of Piastri,* or Crowns. These are his Annual Revenues; besides his Jewels, Forfeitures, and his *Dacii*: which last, are of vast profit to him.

Interest.

The Interest of this Prince is much *Austrian,* and consequently *Spanish*; yet not so far, as to break with *France,* to which he opens his Ports and Passages for his own sake. He loves to have

have no War in *Italy*, becaufe he hath fomething to lofe: and though he loves to have the *Pope* his Friend, yet he cares not for having any of his Subjects *Pope*. A *Pope* of his Family, *Clement* VII. having made him what he is, he is affraid a *Pope* of fome other *Florentine* Family would ftrive to make him what he was.

As for the Language of *Florence*, it's pure, but in their Books, not in their mouths: They do fo choak it in the Throat, that it's almoft quite drown'd there: nor doth it recover it felf again till it come to *Rome*, where *Lingua Tofcana in bocca Romana* is a moft fweet Language. The *Academy of the Crufca*, hath much contributed to the enriching of this Language with choice words. The rich *Dictionary* made by this famous Company, and called from them the *Crufca*, was forty years in compiling, but it will be in *vogue* as long as Men fhall fpeak *Italian*. *The Language.* *The Academy of the Crufca.*

Finally, for the Learned Men of this Town in latter times, they are thefe; *Marfilius Ficinus* the Chriftian Platonick; *Dante* and *Petrarch* in *Poetry*: *Guicciardin* in Hiftory: *Poggio* in raillery: *Vefpucius* in Geography: *Accurfius* in Law: *Michael Angelo* in Painting: *Joannes Cafa* in Practical Morality: *Naclantus* in Divinity: *Galileo* in Aftronomy: *Doni, Luigi, Alemanni*, and others in *Belle Lettere*. *The Learned Men.*

He that defires to know the Hiftory of *Florence*, let him read *Giovanni Villani, Mattheo Villani, Scipione Ammirato*, and the Life of *Gran Cofimo*. *The Hiftorians.*

J. Having

Having thus seen Fair *Florence* we, desired to see *Legorne*, and make an excursive Journey by *Pistoia*, *Lucca* and *Pisa*. *Pistoia*, is an ancient Town in a plain Country. Of this Town was Pope *Clement* the IX. of the ancient Family of *Rospigliosi*: and that is all I can say of it: for it looks baldly of it self, either out of pure old age, else by reason of its Neighbourhood to *Florence*, which hath fleeced it, or, which I rather think, by reason of its Civil Factions heretofore, which had almost quite ruin'd it.

Lucca is a pretty little Common-wealth, and yet it sleeps quietly within the Bosom of the Great Dukes State. But that State may wisely fear none, which no State fears; and the Great Duke may be unwilling to measure his Sword, with that of little *Lucca*, lest the World shou'd cry shame upon him, and bid him meddle with his Match. This little Republick looked in my eye, like a perfect Map of old *Rome* in its beginning. It's governed by a *Confaloniero* and the Gentry. The great Counsel consists of 160 Citizens who are changed every year. It's under the Emperors Protection; and it hath about thirty thousand Souls in it. Approaching unto it, it looked like a pure Low-Country Town, with its Brick Walls, large Ramparts set round with Trees, and deep Moats round about the Walls. It hath eleven Bastions well guarded by the Townsmen, and well furnished with Cannons of a large size. The Town is three miles in compass; it hath thirty thousand Muskets or half Muskets in its *Arsenal*, eight thousand Pikes, two thousand Brest pieces of Musket proof, and store of great Artillery. The whole

whole State, for a need, can arm eighteen thou- *Its Reve-*
sand Men of service, and it hath about five hun- *nues.*
dred thousand *French* Livres a year. It was in
this Town that *Cæsar*, *Pompey*, and *Crassus* met,
and agreed among themselves that all things in
Rome should pass as they pleased.

The chief things to be seen here are the Cathedral, called S. *Martins*, whose Bishop hath
the Ensigns of an Archbishop, to wit, the use of
the *Pallium* and the Cross, and whose Canons in
the Quire wear a Rochet and Camail, and Miters of Silk like Bishops.

2. The *Town-House*, or *Senate-House*, where
the *Confalonitro* lives during the time of his
Charge.

3. The Church of S *Frediano* belonging to the
Canon Regulars, where in a Chapel on the left
hand is the *Tomb of S. Richard King of England*,
who died here in his Pilgrimage to *Rome*.

4 The *Augustins* Church, where is seen a hole
where the Earth opened to swallow up a blas-
pheming Gamester.

Of this Town was Pope *Lucius* III. The two
famous Men of this Town, the one for Soldi-
ery, the other for Learning, were brave *Ca-
strucio*, and *Sanctus Pagninus* a great *Hebrecian*.

There are five Towns more belonging to
Lucca, to wit, *Ca-magior*, *Viareggia*, *Montignoso*,
Castilione, and *Minucciano*.

From *Lucca* we went to *Pisa*, some ten miles *Pisa.*
off. This was once the head Town of a flourishing *Republick*, and then the *Numantia* of *Florence*, and scorning its yoke; but how it crou-
cheth to it, It stands in no very good Air, and
therefore hath been vex'd with divers plagues.

The

The Grafs in the Streets of this *University* read me this Lecture, and I believed it, Whereupon I refolved to ſtay here one day only, in which time I saw,

The Domo. 1. The *Domo*, whofe *Canons* officiate in *Scarlet* like Cardinals. This is a neat Church for ſtructure, and for its three *Brazen Doors* hiſtoried with a fine *Baffo relievo.* It's built after *La maniera Tedeſcha*, a faſhion of Building much uſed in *Italy* four or five hundred years ago, and brought in by *Germans* or *Tedeſchi*, faith *Vafari.*

The bending Tower. 2. Near to the *Domo* ſtands (if leaning may be called *ſtanding*) the *bending Tower*, ſo artificially made, that it ſeems to be falling, and yet it ſtands firm: *Ruituraque ſemper ſtat (mirum) moles.*

3. On the other ſide of the *Domo*, is the *Campo Santo*, a great ſquare place cloiſtered about with a low Cloiſter curiouſly painted. It's called the *Campo Santo*, becauſe therein is conſerved the Holy Earth brought from *Hieruſalem* in 50 Gallies of this Republick, *an.* 1224. Theſe Gallies were ſent by the Republick of *Piſa*, to ſuccour the Emperor *Ænobarbe*, in the *Holy Land*; but hearing of his death when they came thither, they returned home again loaden with the Earth of the *Holy Land*, of which they made this *Campo Santo.*

Some Colleges. 4. Some good *Colleges* there are, but unfrequented then by reaſon of a late Plague: none running faſter from the Plague than Scholars, eſpecially when it comes near to the Schools.

The Library. 5. The publick Library is much enriched with the acceſſion of *Aldus Manutius* his Library.

The Phyſick Garden. 6. The Garden of Simples may be rare; but we not underſtanding this Herb Language, haſted

Part I. A Voyage to ITALY. 149

sted to the House of the *Knights of St. Stephen.*

7. This is the only *Order of Knighthood* that I perceived in *Florence*; and it's very common. They wear a Red Cross of Satin upon their Cloaks, and profess to fight against the *Turks.* For this purpose they have here a good House and Maintenance. Their Church is beautified without with a handsome *Faciata* of *White Marble*, and within with *Turkish Ensigns* and divers *Lanterns* of *Capitanesse Galies*. In this House the *Knights* live in common, and are well maintained. In their *Treasury* they shew you a great *Buckler* all of Pearl and Diamonds, won in a Battle against the *Turks*. Indeed Bucklers of *Diamonds* do but shew our Enemies where we are, and what they may hope for by killing us. They have in their *Cancellaria*, a Catologue of those Knights who have done notable Service against the *Turks*; which serves for a powerful exhortation to their Successors, to do, and die bravely. In fine, these Knights may marry if they will, and live in their own particular Houses, but many of them choose celebacy as more convenient for brave Soldiers; Wives and Children being the true *impedimenta exercitus.*

The Knights of S. Ste. ha-

Heretofore, during the great disorders of the *Guelfs* and the *Ghibelins*, Anno 1282. This Town was governed by *Ugolin* a proud Man, who ruled here despotically. This Man inviting one day all his Friends to a great Feast; began in the midst of it to brag, that nothing was wanting to him: *Yes* (said one of his best Friends, because one who flattered him not) *there's one thing yet wanting to thee*, Ugolin, *to wit, the Anger of God, which is not far from thee.*

And

A **Voyage to** ITALY. Part I.

And it proved true, for presently after, the *Ghibelins* rushing into the Palace of *Ugolin* (chief of the *Guelfs*) killed in his fight, one of his Sons and his Nephew, and taking him with two other of his Sons and three Nephews, they shut him up in a strong Tower, and threw the *Keys* into *Arno*: where the poor Man that bragged even now in a Feast, died soon after of Hunger, having first seen his Children and Nephews die of hunger in his Arms. A rare example to teach proud Men, that there's often but one day between a *powerful* Man and a *poor* Man; between a great *Feast* and a great *Fast*. Here in *Pisa* were called two Councils, the one 1409, the other 1511.

Ligorne. From *Pisa* we went to *Ligorne*, (*Portus Libernus* in *Latin*) through a pleasant Forest. This is the only Haven the *Great Duke* hath; and the mouth which letteth in that food which fatteneth this State. We stayed not long here, the season pressing us to be gone, and the Town being soon seen, for it's but little, though one of the neatest Haven Towns a Man can see. Heretofore it was not sufferable by reason of the bad Air; but since *Ferdinand the first* built it anew, and dryed up the neighbouring Fens (gathering much of the water into a cut Channel, which goes [...] to *Pisa*, and carries great Boats) the Town is twice as wholesome, and thrice as rich as it was.

The things I saw in this Town were these. 1. The *Mole* which shuts up the Haven. 2. The *Lantern* which with seven lights guides in Ships in the night. 3. The *Haven* it self where Ships lie safe, and the *little Haven*, within that, which
serves

Part I. *A Voyage to* ITALY.

serves for a withdrawing Room to the great Haven, where the Galleys themselves retire. 4. The Statue of *Ferdinand* the first in marble, with the *Statue in bronze* of *four slaves* at his feet. These are the 4 slaves that would have stoln away a Galley and have rowed here themselves alone; but were taken in their great enterprize. 5. The *Greek Church*. 6. The *Castle*. 7. The Tower in the Sea where they keep Gunpowder. 8. The Jews Synagogue. 9. Two Windmills which are rare things in *Italy*, and therefore must have a place here among the rarities of this Town.

I found not any Academy of Wits here, nor any Records of any learned Men of this Town. All the *Latin* here is only *Meum* and *Tuum*, and their Wits are exercised here how to make good *Bargains*, not good *Books*. Indeed what should the *Muses* do here amongst the horrible noise of Chains, of Carts, of bawling Sea-men, of clamerous Porters, and where the Slaves of *Barbary* are able to fright all Learning out of the Town with their looks, as all *Latin* with their Language. Yet I must confess they study here *belle Lettere*: for, if the true *belle Lettere* be Letters of Exchange, your Merchant here, if you present him a Letter of Exchange from his Correspondent, will read it over and over again, and study upon it, before he give you the Contents of it in Money.

Having finished this excursive journey, we returned again to *Florence*; and having rested our Horses a day or two, we took a new rise from thence to *Rome*, which seemed to beckon

L 4 us

us, and whither the main Torrent of our curiosity hurried us.

Some three miles beyond *Florence* we passed under a *Monastery* of *Carthusians*, seated upon a round hill, whose several *celles* and little Gardens (walled about) branching out on all sides like several Bastions, made this Monastery look like a spiritual Fort, or devout Cittadel.

San Cassiano.
Poggi Bonzi.

From hence passing through *San Cassiano*, we arrived at night at *Poggi-Bonzi*, a little Town, famous for perfumed *Tabaco* in Powder which the *Italians* and *Spaniards* take far more frequently then we, as needing neither Candle nor Tinderbox to light it withal; nor using any other Pipes than their own Noses.

Siena.

From *Poggi-Fonzi* we came at Dinner to *Siena*. This is the second Town of the *Florentine* State. It was heretofore a powerful Republick, commanding threescore miles into the Country, and now and then beating the *Florentines*: but at last, after much struggling, this *Wolf* received the muzzle, and *Siena* is now the humble servant of *Florence*. This happened *Anno* 1555.

The Arms of Siena are a Wolf.

This Town is seated in a very wholesome Air and Soil, and therefore much frequented by Strangers. It's called *Sena* in Latin, from the *Senones*, people of *Gaul*, who coming into *Italy* with *Brennus*, built this Town. The Streets are all paved with bricks set up edgeway, which makes the Town always dry and neat. It's built high and low, with many high Towers in it, built anciently in honour of it's well deserving Citizens, who had done some special Service in the *Republick*; and this makes

it

Part I. A Voyage to ITALY.

it seen thirty miles off on *Romes* side. The People here are very civil, and even sociable too, which together with the good Air, the good Exercises for Gentlemen, the good Language, and the great Privileges, make many Strangers draw Bridle here, and pass the Summer at *iena*, the *Orleans* of *Italy*.

The prime things I saw here, were these.

1. The *Domo*, one of the neatest Cathedrals of *Italy*, though it be built *a la maniera Tedescha*. It's all of black and white Marble within and without. The Frontispiece is carved curiously and set thick with Statues. Yet it wants a larger Piazza before it, to give it it's full Grace. The inside of this Church is very taking. Under the roof immediately runs a row of white marble heads of all the Popes till this time. The *Pavement* is the best in the World: and indeed too good to be trod on; hence they cover a great part of it, with Broads handsomely laid together, yet easie to be taken up, to shew Strangers the Beauty of it: Its of *Marble* inlaid with Pictures, and those very great ones: several great Marbles of several Colours making the Shadows and the Lights, and composing all together such a new kind of Mosaick work, as all Men admire, but none dare finish. This work was begun by *Duccio*

The Domo.

the *Maccabees*; and the like. I confess I scarce saw any thing in *Italy* which pleased me better than this Pavement. On the left hand (within the Church) stands the *Library*, painted with a rare *Fresco*, which is yet ravishing and lively after two hundred years: Indeed, the brave actions of *Æneas Sylvius*, (afterwards Pope Pius II.) which these Pictures represent, deserve to be painted by the Sun-beams. The Pictures are of the hand of *Pietro Perugino*, *Raphael's Master*: but when all's done, give me Books in a *Library*, not *Pictures*. In the *Church* you see the Statues of *Alexander* the III, of *Pius* II, of *Paulus* V, and of *Alexander* the VII, all Popes, and Natives of *Siena*.

The Library.

S. Katerine of Siena.

2. I saw here the several places which S. *Katherine* of *Siena* had made famous by her Devotions: as, her Chamber, where she received the holy *Stigmata*, now turned into a Chapel: the Chamber where she lived, with other memorials of her Devotions, in the *Dominicans* Church; where they also shew her Head and Finger: her Body being transferred to *Rome*, and lying in a little Chapel within the Sacristy of the *Dominicans*, at the *Minerva*.

Other Rarities.

3. The other things ordinarily shown here are the great Hospital: the House of *Pius* II. of the Family of the *Piccolomoni*: the great Piazza: the Pillar with the Wolf of Brass upon it: the Marble Pillar as you come into the Town from *Florence*, with the Arms of the Empire and of *Portugal* upon it; because here it was that the Emperor met *Eleonora* of *Portugal*, and married her in presence of *Æneas Sylvius* then Archbishop here, and afterwards Pope *Pius* the II.   4. I

he Academy of Wits, called *gli In-* *The Acade-*
 should take that ambitious name *my of Wits.*
Is it be in reference to the saying of
 said, that then finally Kingdoms
when either Philosophers should be
 Kings played the Philosophers,
holds, that they that are strong of
 serve and tug at the Oar of Com-
that are strong in wit, are born by
e Helm, and command others.
 hath furnished the Latin Church
Councel of an hundred and thirty
Nicolas III. with three great Saints,
former of the *Minorites*; St. *Ka-*
Virgin, and *Beatus Columbanus*, in-
rder of the *Jesuati*, said to be a
rning and Sanctity: with four *Popes*
er III. of the House of *Bandinelli*;
louse of *Piccolomini*; *Paulus* V. of
rgesi; and *Alexander* VII. of the
And in fine, it hath furnished the
 Champions in Learning *Ambrosius*
rinus) who wrote against *Luther* —
nd *Adriano Politi*, who wrote a-
by his Learned Dictionary.
ld know the particular History of *The Bills*-
d *Orlando Malevolto*. *ry.*
e want to *Bon Convento*, *Tornieri*,
considerable places upon the rode, *Podiersc.*
no, a strong Castle upon a high Hill,
ius King of the *Longobards*. This
f the *Florentine* State, but not the

: the Great Dukes Inn at the bottom
ent to lodge at *Aquapendente*, which *Aquapen-*
 off, and the first Town of the Popes *dente.*

Town is made a Bishops Seat by the demonlishment of *Castro*, and the removal of the Bishops Seat from thence hither, which hath happened upon this occasion. *Castro* was a Town belonging to the Duke of *Parma*, thither Pope *Innocent* X. sent a good Bishop to govern that Flock; but the Bishop, upon his arrival being killed there, the Pope sent *Conte Vidman* (General then of the Church) with order to demolish *Castro*: and he himself transferred the Bishops Seat from thence to *Aquapendente*, all which was, according to the Canon Law, which ordains, that the City which kills its Bishop should be deprived of the Bishops Seat ever after.

From *Aquapendente* we came to a little Town called *San Lorenzo*, and not long after to *Bolsena*, anciently called *Urbs Volsinensium*. Here it was that we were told of a famous Miracle, that they give out to have been done in this place, in confirmation of the real presence of Christs Body and Blood in the Sacrament, which happened Anno 1263, and which gave occasion to Pope *Urban* IV. to command that the Feast of *Corpus Christi* should be kept Holy-day, ever after. The Miracle is related by *Leandro Alberti* the *Camden* of *Italy*, and by *Onuphrius Panvinius*, in the Life of *Urban* IV.

We passed also that morning by the side of the Lake of *Bolsena*; in the middle of which is a little Island, in which *Amalasuinta* Queen of the *Ostrogoths*, a Woman of singular parts, was miserably murthered by her nearest kindred. Heres also a little Convent of *Capuchins*.

Having passed along this Lake a great while, we entered at last into a Wood called anciently *Lucus Volsinensium*, and now, *Bosco Hiberno*. It was formerly a dangerous Passage for Bandito's: but now it's free from danger, since *Sixtus Quintus* purg'd the Ecclesiastical State of that Vermin, by making a Law, that whosoever should bring in the head of a Bandito, should have pardon, impunity and recompense too, of some hundreds of Crowns; whereupon the Bandits soon destroyed one another.   From

od we soon came to *Montefiascone* Montefia-
Hill. It's a Bishops Seat, and *scone*.
lent *Muscatelo* Wine ; and this
for having killed a *Dutchman* here
uch of it. The Story is true, and
nan of Condition travelling thro'
n before him always, with a charge
Inns where the best Wine was,
ipon the Wall of the Inn the word
say, *Here it is.* The Servant co-
le before his Master, and finding
ently good, wrote upon the Wall
T, signifying thereby the super-
of this Wine. The Master arrives,
ns hand-writing ; and finding three
oyed. In he goes, and resolves to
ie did so indeed : for here he lies
t in Wine, and then in his Grave ;
so much of this good Wine, he
was buried by his Servant, in a
ow the Hill, with this Epitaph up-
iade by the same Servant, *Propter*
rus meus mortuus est. It was here
jallantry of the brave *Roman* Ge-
ppeared very much. For, while he
his Town, called then *Phaliscum* or
reacherous School-Master, having
im the chief young Youths of the
he had deceitfully drawn unto the
under pretence of taking the Air a-
h means *Camillus* might have, fright-

Roman Generosity, submmitted willingly to *Camillus*, who had chosen rather to take Towns by his own Valour than by other Mens iniquity: Indeed, (as *Valerius Maximus* saith) it did not become *Rome*, built by the Son of *Mars*, to take Towns otherwise than Martially.

Viterbo. From *Montefiascone* we went down the Hill by an easie descent unto *Viterbo*. This is an Episcopal Seat, standing in a wholesome Air, and therefore called *Viterbium*, as it were, *Vita Urbium*. Here are excellent Fountains of Water, and store of them: but it's pity none of them run with good Wine, to make amends for the bad, which are most of them *Vini cotti*. The two Factions here of the *Gatti* and the *Maganesi*, (these standing for the *Ursini*, those for the *Colonesi*) ruined heretofore *Viterbo* over and over again. In the *Domo* there are the Tombs of four Popes, as also in the *Franciscans* Church some Tombs of Popes and of St. *Rosa*: you see the body of that Saint yet entire, though buried above 100 years ago. She lies along in her Tomb, and is seen by drawing of a Curtain from before her.

The Academy of Wits. Here's an Academy of Wits called *Gli Ostinati*, to shew perchance, that a Man cannot be learned without obstinate labour and pains. Hence the Poet makes the Learned Man to be one who *multum sudavit & alsit*: and *Persius* tells us, that his delight was to grow pale with obstinate night Study: *Velle suum cuique est*, &c.

At me nocturnis juvat impallescere chartis.

About a mile from *Viterbo* stands a neat Church and Convent, called *Madonna del Querca*, and as far again beyond that, a fine House, with a Garden of Water-works and Fountains, worth seeing.

Caprarola. From *Viterbo* (being upon our own Horses) we went to see *Caprarola*, a stately House belonging to the Duke of *Parma*. The House is held to be one of the finest in *Italy* for Architecture. It stands

le out of the Travellers rode, but not of his
for it's much in a Mans way to see such a
 House as this. It stands upon the side of a
 nd from one of the Balconies it shews you *Rome*
two and thirty miles off. It's built in a *Pen-*
 (if I remember well) without, and round
n. The Chambers for all that are square;
well proportioned. The chief of these Cham-
ure painted by the hand of *Pietro Orbista*, flou-
 ig thus upon the noble actions of *Paulus* III.
 ng the other Chambers, the whispering Cham-
 s curious, for four Men here standing, each
 n one of the four corners of this great Cham-
hear distinctly what any of them whispers in
 tone in his Corner, their Faces being turn-
) the Wall; and yet those that stand in the
 t of the Chamber cannot hear it. The other
 mber is no less curious, where, standing in
 nidst of it, and stamping hard with your foot
 : that are without at the door think that they
 the cracks, or reports of Pistols. The other
 ms here also, as the Kitchin, all of one Stone;
 low Cave also with the Pillar in it, cut like-
 : out of a rock and bearing up the whole Pave-
 t of the round Court which lets light into this
 e by divers round grates of Iron, are worth the
 olding: Then the Garden upon the Hill-side with
 great variety of Water-works, Grots and wet-
 , sports, are all curious things. Having wal-
 this Garden about, you'll desire after so much
 iter, a little Wine, which will not be wanting
 ou, from the rare Cellar lying under the great
 rasse before the House; and perchance you'll
 ik the Wine-works here as fine as the Water-
 rks.
 rom *Caprarola* we fell into our way again at *Mon-* Monter

rofus, from the carrying about with them in Carts, all their goods.) Near to *Bacan* is a Lake out of which runs the River *Varea,* anciently called *Cremera,* near unto which the *Veientes* killed in one Battle, three hundred *Fabii,* that is, the whole family of the *Fabii,* (who had vowed themselves to death for the Common-Wealth service) except one little boy not able to bear arms, from whom *Fabius Maximus* the terror of *Hannibal,* and *Romes* buckler descended.

Varea.

Veii.

Upon this rode also stood anciently the Town *Veii,* a Town which held out ten Summers against the *Romans,* and stood in need of no less Man than *Camillus* to take it. This Town was once so great that *Rome* being destroyed almost by the *Gauls,* the Senators held a Consultation in the *Comitium,* whether they should retire to *Veii,* and leave *Rome* quite, or rebuild again *Romes* walls; but during this Consultation, the Troops returning out of Garrison, arrived by chance into the *Comitium,* where the Centurion entring, and not thinking the Senators had been there, cryed out to the Standerd-bearer, *Signifer starne signum, hic optime manebimus;* which words the Senators hearing, cryed out to one another, *Accipimus omen;* and presently laid aside all further thought of retiring to *Veii.*

Valer. Max, l. 1. c. 5.

Some twelve miles before we came to *Rome,* we saw the *Cupola* of St. *Peters* Church, and were as glad to see it afar off, as the weary *Trojans* in *Æneas* his Company, were glad to see *Italy,* after so much wandering. Some few hours after, having passed by an old Tomb, which some call *Nero's* Tomb; and over the *Ponte Molo* (of which more in my 2. Part), we entred into *Rome* by the *Via Flaminea,* and *Porta del Populo.*

The End of the first Part.

www.ingramcontent.com/pod-product-compliance
Lightning Source LLC
Chambersburg PA
CBHW032144160426
43197CB00008B/769